Inside Information

Developing Powerful Readers and Writers of Informational Text Through Project-Based Instruction

Nell K. Duke

SCHOLASTIC

New York • Toronto • London • Auckland • Sydney
Mexico City • New Delhi • Hong Kong • Buenos Aires

To Julia and Cooper

Credits: p. 46: illustration created by Red King Creative LLC and used by permission. p. 60: description of lesson used by permission of Tara Kras; p. 61: From *Early Intervention for Reading Difficulties: The Interactive Strategies Approach* (p. 61), by D.M. Scanlon, K. L. Anderson, and J. M. Sweeney, 2010. New York: The Guilford Press. Copyright, 2010 by the Guilford Press. Reprinted with permission. p. 64: illustration created by Red King Creative LLC and used by permission. p. 81: From *Improving Reading Comprehension in Kindergarten Through 3rd Grade: A Practice Guide* (p. 20), by T. Shanahan, K. Callison, C. Carriere, N. K. Duke, P. D. Pearson, C. Schatschneider, and J. Torgesen, 2010, Washington, D.C: National Center for Education and Evaluation and Regional Assistance, Institute of Education Sciences, U.S. Department of Education. p. 83: From "Diagrams, Timelines, and Tables—Oh, My!" by Kathryn L. Roberts, Rebecca R. Norman, Nell K. Duke, Paul Morsink, Nicole M. Martin, and Jennifer A. Knight, 2013, *The Reading Teacher*, 61, pp. 16–18. Copyright 2013 by the International Reading Association. Reprinted with permission. p. 98: From "Essential Elements of Fostering and Teaching Reading Comprehension" by Nell K. Duke, P. D. Pearson, S. L. Strachan, and A. K. Billman, 2011. In S. J. Samuels and A. E. Farstrup (Eds.), *What Research Has to Say About Reading Instruction* (4th ed.) (p. 65), Newark, DE: International Reading Association. Copyright 2011 by the International Reading Association. Reprinted with permission. pp. 122, 136: From *Teaching Elementary School Students to Be Effective Writers: A Practice Guide* (pp. 16, 18) by S. Graham, A. Bollinger, C. Booth Olson, C. D'Aoust, C. MacArthur, D. McCutheon, and N. Olinghouse, 2012, Washington, D.C: National Center for Education and Evaluation and Regional Assistance, Institute of Education Sciences, U.S. Department of Education. p. 123: illustration created by Edward Coutu and used by permission. p. 140: From *Beachcombing* by Jim Arnosky. Copyright 2004 by Jim Arnosky. Used by permission of Dutton Children's Books. p. 145: (top) From *Biblioburro: A True Story From Colombia* by Jeanette Winter. Copyright 2010 by Jeanette Winter. Used by permission of Scholastic, Inc. (middle) From "Olympians vs. Animals," by Sara Goudarzi. Copyright 2014 by Scholastic, Inc. Used by permission of Scholastic, Inc. (bottom) From *When Marian Sang: The True Recital of Marian Anderson, the Voice of a Century* by Pam Muñoz Ryan. Text copyright 2002 by Pam Muñoz Ryan. Illustrations copyright 20012 by Brian Selznick. Used by permission of Scholastic, Inc. pp. 184–185, 186: From "Improving the School Reading Program: A New Call for Collaboration" by S. Walpole and K. Najera, 2013. In B. M. Taylor and N. K. Duke (Eds.), *Handbook of Effective Literacy Instruction: Research-Based Practice K–8*, (pp. 517–518, 525), New York: The Guilford Press. Copyright 2013 by the Guilford Press. Reprinted with permission. Every effort has been made to find the authors and publishers of previously published material in this book and to obtain permission to print it.

PHOTO CREDITS: Photo Editor: Cynthia Carris. Photos ©: Alamy Images—p. 33: Harvey (Portrait Essentials), Fleming (Pictorial Press Ltd), McClintock (PF-bygone1), Pasteur (The Print Collector), p. 96: bottom left (Tony Morris/Jason Smalley Photo), p. 145: center left (Doug Perrine); Clean Slate Press (Amy Lam)—p. 83: timelines, p. 143: all photos, p. 179; Collaborative Productions (John Scollon)—cover and pp. 14, 51, 58, 129, 130, 139, 157, 164, 168; Corbis Images—p. 142: bottom (Bettmann), p. 145: center right (Christian Liewig); David Ammer—p. 83: insets (2); Dreamstime/Gunold Brunbauer—p. 54: center; Fotolia—p. 53: bottom right (2436digitalavenue), p. 141 (XXII); Getty Images—p. 33: Anning (The Bridgeman Art Library), p. 53: bottom left (Michael Patrick O'Neill), p. 56: heart (Brian Evans/Photo Researchers); iStockphoto—p. 54: left (yenwen), right (Casarsa), p. 57: plates and silverware (Sitade), p. 105 (33karen33); Melissa Winchell—p. 83: diagram: cross-section, diagram: surface (from Alison K. Billman and Katherine R. Hilden [2008], p.17; PDF available at http://msularc. educ.msu.edu/coca-materials); National Cancer Institute—p. 33: Elion; Scholastic, Inc.—p. 83: captioned graphic (Greg Harris), flowchart and map (Maria Lilja), graph (Andrea Tachiera), table (Adrienne Downey), p. 102: puppets (Maria Lilja); Shutterstock, Inc.—p. 56: pizza (Aaron Amat), p. 57: napkin (Constantine Pankin), glass (Givaga); Thinkstock—p. 33: bottom left (Heinrich Volschenk), p. 53: background (iStockphoto), p. 56: cupcake (Ruth Black), fries (Maceofoto), salt shaker (Viktor Fischer); p. 95: top right (Anatoliy Babiy), p. 96: bottom right (Oleksii Sergieiev), top left (View Stock); United States Patent & Trademark Office—p. 142: top; USDA/choosemyplate.gov—p. 56: calorie graph.

Cover Design: Maria Lilja
Interior Design: Red King Creative LLC
Cover Photograph: Collaborative Productions
Development Editor: Raymond Coutu
Production Editor: Sarah Glasscock
Copy Editor: David Klein
ISBN: 978-0-545-66768-5
Copyright © 2014 by Nell K. Duke
All rights reserved.
Printed in the U.S.A.

4   5   6   7   8   9   10   31   20   19   18   17

CONTENTS

FOREWORD

I have always been fascinated by students' desire to identify problems and work toward solutions. All children are hard-wired to be problem solvers, I believe. They long to understand, are often troubled by issues in their communities, and are driven to be part of the solution.

Six-year-old Hannah listened intently as I read Mem Fox's *Wilfrid Gordon McDonald Partridge*, in which a boy helps some elderly neighbors "find their memories" by salvaging artifacts to share—objects that trigger recollections and lovely stories. When I gave all the children a moment to turn and talk about the book, I noticed Hannah turn to Luke and say, "We gotta get over there right now!" I had no idea what she was talking about, but she was quite intent on "getting over there," wherever "there" was.

I soon learned that an assisted-living facility was situated just two blocks from the school. Hannah wanted to "get over there" to help the elderly residents find their memories! Wilfrid Gordon McDonald Partridge had shown the way, and she was determined to follow his lead. Her teacher formed a "study group" that delved into issues facing the elderly, including Alzheimer's disease. Eventually, a band of nine first graders, armed with knowledge about senior citizens and objects to trigger their memories, marched up the street and made new friends. Hannah was right. They needed to get over there!

The urgency the children felt was palpable that day. They felt responsible for, and capable of, making an important contribution in their community. Hannah's determination was contagious. I'm certain that, to this day, those children remember what they learned and the impact they had on their neighbors. The drive came from them; the engagement was undeniable.

Though we didn't call it project-based learning, that's exactly what it was. The idea could have come from the teacher, but it didn't. It came from Hannah. The initiative could have been on any number of topics, but the children chose to help senior citizens reclaim memories. A real-world issue came into view, and the children informed themselves and acted! They left the facility with written and illustrated evidence of their concern and new knowledge of issues facing elderly people.

Project-based learning, as Nell Duke describes it in *Inside Information*, is not your mother's thematic unit or genre study. Nell clearly differentiates among these approaches and makes a strong case for a project-based approach. She describes the research-based tactics we can use to address standards, while capitalizing on students' interests, family assets, and real-world problems in need of solutions.

Inside Information encourages us to join students in taking a closer look at the world outside of school in search of vexing problems. Nell shows how students can read and research, write, and ultimately make real contributions in the world.

I must say that *Inside Information* surprised me a bit. I expected to read about engaging students in informational text and authentic inquiry projects. But this book is about much more than that. Nell describes great instructional practices that can (and should) be applied in nearly every learning context. Her discussion of conducting read-alouds, using the gradual release of responsibility model, and teaching text structures and features, for example, are simply best practices that can guide instruction in any discipline.

I was also quite curious to see who might benefit most from this book and was delighted to learn that it is for us all! I know experienced teachers will use it to remind themselves to focus instruction on what matters most. They will find affirmation as well as new thinking—a clear path through the cacophony of mandates and quick-fix ideas with which we educators are barraged.

I can just as easily imagine early-career educators inhaling this book and returning to it frequently. They will come to understand the importance of young learners having a clear sense of purpose and audience, and of creating authentic learning experiences. As teachers, these are among the most important lessons we can ever learn.

Because of Nell's encyclopedic knowledge of research, her familiarity with classrooms, and her own (often hilarious) experiences as a parent, she brings authority to her message. I've come to appreciate her wisdom through our years of co-editing, planning institutes and workshops, the occasional healthy argument, and friendship. I am delighted that you, too, will benefit from that wisdom as you help your students delve inside information!

Ellin Oliver Keene

PREFACE The Rise of Informational Text, or Be Careful What You Wish For!

Colleagues and I published our first articles arguing for greater attention to informational text in elementary education in 1998 (Caswell & Duke, 1998; Duke & Kays, 1998; Kays & Duke, 1998). In 2000, I published a study documenting that a mere 3.6 minutes per day of instructional time in first-grade classrooms involved informational text, and even less—1.4 minutes per day—in low socioeconomic status (SES) school districts. In the decade that followed, I saw many signs that attention to informational text was on the rise, for example in the degree to which publishers were producing and selling informational text for young children, but in actual classroom practice, attention to informational text at the elementary school level remained lower than I thought it should be (e.g., Jeong, Gaffney, & Choi, 2010; R. H. Yopp & H. K. Yopp, 2006).

The Rise of Informational Text

Then came the Common Core State Standards (CCSS) (National Governors Association Center for Best Practices & Council of Chief State School Officers, 2010). The CCSS have specific standards for reading informational text and writing informative/explanatory text beginning at kindergarten. The standards expect a large proportion of elementary-school students' reading and writing to be of informational text. Specifically, they draw from the National Assessment of Educational Progress (NAEP) 2009 Framework in calling for 50% informational reading in fourth grade (the elementary grade level at which NAEP is administered) (p. 5). The standards imply that this is the expectation across the elementary grades: "In K–5, the Standards follow NAEP's lead in balancing the reading of literature with the reading of informational texts" (p. 5). Similarly, the CCSS follow the NAEP 2011 Framework in calling for 35% of fourth-grade students' writing to be informative/explanatory and 30% to be persuasive (p. 5), an enormous increase over what has historically been expected.

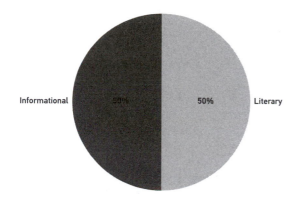

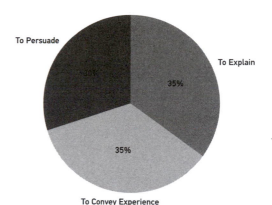

FIGURE 1.1: Distribution of literary and informational passages in Grade-4 2009 NAEP Reading Framework

FIGURE 1.2: Distribution of communicative purposes in Grade-4 2011 NAEP Writing Framework

The CCSS include many different kinds of text under the umbrella of "informational text": "Biographies"; "Autobiographies"; "Books about history, social studies, science, and the arts," which I assume means informative/explanatory texts, texts that present arguments in these areas, and, perhaps, nonfiction narrative/true-story texts on these topics; "Technical texts, including directions [what I call *procedural* or *how-to* text], forms, and information displayed in graphs, charts, or maps"; and "Digital sources on a range of topics" (p. 31). If you are familiar with my previous work (e.g., Duke & Bennett-Armistead, 2003), you will notice that this is a broader use of the term *informational text* than I had used. Given the reach of the CCSS, I have adopted their broader use of the term.

Rather than using "informational text," for writing the CCSS use the terms:

- "informative/explanatory text" (Standard 2)

- "opinion" (Standard 1, elementary grades)

- "argument" (Standard 1, middle- and high-school grades)

The latter two are examples of writing "to persuade" (p. 5).

When designing instruction, and in this book, I usually break "informational text" into five types, each of which has a different purpose:

- **Informative/explanatory:** to convey information about the natural or social world

- **Persuasive:** to influence the reader's ideas or behaviors
  Note: I prefer the term "persuasive" over "argumentative" for several reasons, including that it emphasizes the text purpose—to persuade—and that it seems to more naturally include a broader range of texts that are commonly found in the workplace and society.

- **Nonfiction narrative:** to interpret and share the story of a real event
  Note: Many nonfiction narratives, such as a story of what I did over the weekend, should not be considered "informational text" in my opinion. Others, such as an information-rich account of the voyage of the *Titanic*, perhaps could be considered "informational text," and are, in CCSS terms (p. 31).

- **Biography:** to interpret and share the experiences of a real person

- **Procedural:** to teach someone how to do something

Each of these five types of text has not only different purposes, but also different text features. For example, although procedural texts typically have a materials or an ingredients section and a set of ordered steps, persuasive texts do not. Although nonfiction narratives and many biographies are organized chronologically, informative/explanatory texts are typically organized topically. Perhaps not surprisingly, given that texts have different purposes and features, studies suggest that different kinds of text are written and read differently (Duke & Roberts, 2010; Martin, 2011; Olinghouse & Wilson, 2013). And there are instructional techniques that are well suited to some and not to others (Duke & Watanabe, 2013). Throughout this book, you will see ways in which I suggest differentiating instruction for different types of informational text. For example, rather than approaching feedback and revision in the same way for every type of text, in Chapter Six I talk about approaching revision differently, depending upon the text type in which students are writing.

NONFICTION IS NOT A GENRE

I have read and heard many people refer to nonfiction as a genre. Nonfiction is not a genre. Whether genres are defined by their purpose—which is the current preference in the field—or by their form and features, or both, there are many nonfiction genres. For example, a story about what I did over the weekend is nonfiction, but it has a different purpose and different form and features, and is read differently, than an informative/explanatory text about, say, different kinds of things people do on weekends. In fact, in many respects nonfiction narrative has more in common with fictional narrative than with informative/explanatory text. I encourage you to go beyond the label of "nonfiction" to more specific categories of text in your teaching and to be highly skeptical of professional development that refers to "the nonfiction genre."

Be Careful What You Wish For!

You might think that I would be thrilled with the greater attention to informational text that the CCSS are bringing. I am, in a way, but I am also experiencing a bad case of "be careful what you wish for." I am seeing a lot of instructional mistakes and misconceptions about using informational text with elementary-age children. When I called for greater opportunities for students to read and write informational text, I did not mean:

- Handing students difficult books on topics that may or may not be of interest

- Requiring students to write "reports" and "persuasive essays" for no particular reason other than satisfying a school requirement

- Carrying out informational read-alouds no differently from fictional narrative read-alouds

- Asking students a barrage of low-level questions about informational text content

- Having students spend time developing "conventions notebooks" about informational text rather than actually using those conventions to achieve real communicative purposes

- Administrators focusing rigidly on the percentage of informational text teachers are using, with little regard to the content of those texts or how they are being used

- And many other practices I am seeing in the name of informational text instruction

I do understand why this is happening. Most of us got little training in teaching with informational text in our pre-service education. Many of us have experienced little or no professional development on the topic. And, in general, researchers, publishers, and administrators have been slow to meet the pressing needs in this area. I hope that this book can play some small part in helping us move toward higher quality informational reading and writing instruction.

Concluding Thoughts: Informational Text and Project-Based Instruction—a Great Match

Informational text has long been neglected in U.S. elementary classrooms. Although I welcome a move toward greater use of informational text, this move must be made carefully. In the remainder of this book, I focus on an approach—project-based instruction—that I believe may help us to avoid many of the potential pitfalls of informational reading and writing instruction. I believe that project-based instruction is particularly well suited to informational text. Projects often involve solving a problem, addressing a need, or answering a question; these are purposes for reading informational text. Projects often involve conveying solutions to problems, using text to address needs, and communicating answers to questions; these are purposes for writing informational text. This is not to say that project-based instruction cannot be used with non-informational genres. (See, for example, Duke, Caughlan, Juzwik, and Martin, 2012, for a sampling of projects teachers have carried out with literary and dramatic genres.) But it is to say that project-based instruction is a great match for informational texts.

CHAPTER ONE The Power of Project-Based Instruction

I have been studying how children learn to read and write informational text for over 20 years. I have observed in many classrooms, talked with many teachers and students, and read and carried out many research studies. In the process, I have become convinced that a project-based approach is the best overall framework for teaching the reading and writing of informational text. This book will help you learn to develop and implement project-based units for teaching informational reading and writing. I take you step-by-step through the process that I and others have used to design such units. I ask you to start by developing and teaching just one project-based unit. Even with all the wrinkles that come with teaching something for the first time, and all the challenges that project-based teaching can present, I believe developing and teaching one unit like this will sell you on project-based teaching—you will find that it is a more effective, compelling, and invigorating way to teach students to read and write informational text.

What Is a Project-Based Approach to Instruction?

In a project-based approach, students work over an extended time period for a purpose beyond satisfying a school requirement—to build something, to create something, to respond to a question they have, to solve a real problem, or to address a real need. For example, students might work to plan, plant, and cultivate a garden to help feed the hungry in their community; they might develop a guidebook for visitors at a nature preserve; they might study and then develop a plan to reduce waste in the school cafeteria; or they might research and write a history of their local community. Along the way, teachers build knowledge and teach skills, but in students' minds, the knowledge and skills serve to meet the project's goal (while in the teacher's mind, they may also serve to address specific state standards, meet district curriculum requirements, and so on).

Project-based learning is typically interdisciplinary. For example, developing a guidebook for visitors at a nature preserve may involve work commonly associated with social studies, such as surveying visitors about their interests and researching the history of the preserve, as well as work commonly associated with science, such as observing and describing plant and animal life in the preserve. Projects often involve a great deal of reading and writing, as in the guidebook project, for instance, which could entail writing surveys; reading, analyzing, and writing up the survey results; reading and synthesizing historical documents about the preserve; recording observations; and writing the guidebook itself. Oral and written communication with people involved in the project outside of the classroom, such as the ranger of the preserve, is common. Within the classroom, considerable speaking and listening is typically required as students work together to achieve project goals. These days, using a wide range of technological tools is also common in project-based contexts.

PROJECT-BASED INSTRUCTION, PAST AND PRESENT

Project-based approaches have been around for many decades. In the early 1900s, scholars such as John Dewey and William Heard Kilpatrick argued that learning by doing and making instruction purposeful for children would result in more powerful learning (e.g., Dewey, 1902; Kilpatrick, 1918).

Although project-based approaches have been around for a long time, I believe four factors make the time especially ripe for project-based learning. First, as you will see throughout this book, project-based approaches are particularly well suited to addressing the Common Core State Standards for English Language Arts and Literacy in History/Social Studies, Science, and Technical Subjects (National Governors Association Center for Best Practices & Council of Chief State School Officers, 2010).

Second, the skills entailed in project-based learning are consistent with the so-called "21st century skills," skills that are in demand for work and citizenship, such as those identified by the Partnership for 21st Century Skills (http://www.p21.org), including:

- Creativity and Innovation

- Critical Thinking and Problem Solving

- Communication and Collaboration

- Flexibility and Adaptability

- Initiative and Self-Direction

- Social and Cross-Cultural Skills

- Productivity and Accountability

- Leadership and Responsibility

Third, research is increasingly showing that project-based approaches, and their components, improve students' knowledge, skills, and attitudes toward learning. For example, project-based approaches typically involve students in reading and writing for specific purposes beyond just learning to read and write or satisfying school requirements. Research suggests that this is associated with stronger reading and writing growth. Moreover, project-based approaches often involve writing for specific audiences beyond members of the classroom. Again, research suggests that students actually write better under those circumstances. (See also "Does Project-Based Instruction Work?" on pages 16–18.)

Fourth, project-based approaches are more engaging than many traditional kinds of instruction, as the table on page 15 shows. Although motivation and engagement in schooling have always been important, they are more important than ever. Why? Standards expect much more from students than in the past—to get students to engage in the hard, cognitive work necessary to meet these demanding standards, they need to be motivated and engaged in their learning. And current practices may not be motivating or engaging. For example, a meta-analysis (i.e., a study of studies) showed that using the writing process was effective in building writing skills but had no impact on students' motivation to write (Graham & Sandmel, 2011). We need to enact instructional approaches that do positively affect motivation and engagement, as well as achievement. (Note, I recommend using a writing-process approach within project-based units, as well as other instructional methods, as you'll see in Chapters

Five and Six.) This is not only because of more demanding standards but also because of unprecedented competition for students' attention from multimedia entertainment. We simply have to make teaching and learning more interesting for students than we have in the past. Fortunately, research on the importance of motivation and engagement in learning has expanded and grown more compelling. We understand more than ever about how motivation and engagement affect learning and what practices motivate and engage students. Look for tips on supporting motivation and engagement throughout this book.

Kindergarten students celebrate their project—"Kids Saving the Rainforest" picture book—by nurturing a seedling to plant in their community.

TABLE 1: HOW PROJECT-BASED LITERACY INSTRUCTION DIFFERS FROM TRADITIONAL LITERACY INSTRUCTION

Traditional Literacy Instruction	Project–Based Literacy Instruction
Students read, write, and learn because you told them to, their families want them to, and/or they think they should.	Students read, write, and learn because there is a real-world problem to solve, a need to address, or a question to answer.
Students attend to lessons because they're supposed to.	Students attend to lessons because doing so will help them achieve their project goal.
Students complete their homework to obtain a sticker or avoid negative consequences.	Students complete their homework because it helps them get one step closer to their project goal.
Each student works on his or her own writing, which may be unrelated to that of his or her classmates.	Whether writing individually or collaboratively, students work together toward a common writing goal.
Reading, writing, and each content area are taught in different parts of the day.	Reading, writing, and one or more content areas are often integrated.
Students read discrete texts largely unrelated to each other.	Students read many texts on the same topic or closely related topics.
Students read informational text because they were asked to do so.	Students read informational text because they want or need information.
Students write informational text for implicit purposes, for you, their classmates, and perhaps themselves.	Students write informational text for explicit purposes and for audiences beyond the classroom.
Students revise for a better grade.	Students revise to communicate more clearly and convincingly to their audience.
Students revise and edit because they are in the revising and editing phase of the writing process.	Students revise and edit because they want their work to be as credible and polished as possible for their audience.
Students are tested on what they have learned.	Students apply what they have learned.
Students look forward to receiving a grade on their writing.	Students look forward to sharing their writing with the target audience.
Students learn to read and write.	Students learn to affect the world around them through reading and writing.

BUT SHOULDN'T STUDENTS GET TO CHOOSE THEIR OWN GENRES AND TOPICS?

One of the most common concerns I hear about project-based instruction is that it imposes a particular genre and topic for reading and writing on students rather than allowing them to be creative and write about what they want to write about. I have several responses to this concern:

- Project-based instruction does not necessarily take over the entire school day, so there are other parts of the day when there can be more choice in the kinds of reading and writing students do.

- Sometimes wide-open choice can actually be unnatural, overwhelming, and unmotivating for students. How often do you just sit down to write whatever you want to write? How would you feel if faced with that prospect? Many students welcome a specific purpose and audience for their reading and writing.

- It is often possible for students to exercise choice—and almost always possible for them to exercise creativity—within the context of the project. For example, if students are writing articles about animals for a magazine that will be placed in the waiting room of a local doctor's office, they might choose the animal about which they write and how they want to approach the writing. If students are writing a brochure about fun things to do in the community for guests at a local hotel, they might choose the activities they write about and the rhetorical devices they use in their writing. This kind of choice within a topic and task has strong support in research (e.g., Guthrie, McRae, & Klauda, 2007).

Does Project-Based Instruction Work?

Research on project-based learning suggests positive impacts on academic achievement, attitudes, self-efficacy, engagement, and motivation (see reviews by Thomas, 2000 and at http://www.edutopia.org/pbl-research-learning-outcomes). Many studies have examined students' learning and attitudes about learning after experiencing project-based units of instruction (e.g., Filippatou & Kaldi, 2010; Hertzog, 2007; Kaldi, Filippatou, & Govaris, 2011; Okolo & Ferretti, 1996; Rivet & Krajcik, 2004), finding that students developed knowledge, skills, and improved attitudes about learning. Some studies have compared the learning of students who were taught using a project-based approach to that of students who were taught using more traditional instruction. For example, Pedro Hernandez-Ramos and Susan De La Paz (2009) studied eighth graders' learning about the Westward expansion and their attitudes related to that learning. One group of students experienced a project-based approach in which they created documentaries on the topic. The other group experienced more traditional forms of instruction. Pre-/post-assessments of content knowledge, attitudes, and engagement revealed that students experiencing the project-based approach had developed greater content knowledge and reported much higher engagement in learning history than students in the traditional instruction group. Students who experienced the project-based approach also demonstrated greater historical reasoning skills and learned more complex information related to the topic. (See also Parker et al., 2011, in civics and government and Boaler, 1998, in mathematics.)

Some teachers and administrators with whom I have talked have the idea that project-based learning is for older students or gifted students. Some in high-poverty districts have told me that this kind of teaching "just isn't practical for our students." The research so far does not support these positions. The studies cited in the previous paragraph include first graders through high school students, students with learning disabilities, and students in high-poverty school settings. In fact, in a study of a project-based approach to teaching social studies and content literacy to second graders, my colleagues and I were able to close the gap, statistically speaking, between students in high-poverty school districts—who experienced project-based units—and students in wealthy school districts—who did not—on standards-based measures of social studies and content literacy (Halvorsen et al., 2012). Although that study was small in scale, it is certainly promising with respect to the use of project-based approaches with young children in high-poverty settings. (We are currently conducting a related study on a much larger scale; I expect to post results about the project on my website: http://umich.edu/~nkduke/.) For more about research supporting project-based approaches for teaching reading and writing of informational text, see Chapter Two.

Of course, like any approach, project-based instruction has its downsides. Preparing project-based units can take time and effort, though I offer many suggestions in this book, particularly in Chapter Eight, to address that concern. Teachers and students need considerable support to engage effectively in this form of teaching and learning (Thomas, 2000). There is a danger, for example, of getting so wrapped up in completing a project that actual instruction, carefully aligned to standards and students' needs, falls by the wayside. As with any approach, project-based instruction can be implemented well or implemented poorly. This book is designed to put you on the road to high-quality implementation of project-based instruction with informational text.

Where Does Project-Based Instruction Fit in the School Day and Year?

As noted earlier, project-based instruction is often interdisciplinary, and it often involves both reading and writing (as well as speaking and listening). So where does it fit in the school day? Science time? Social studies time? Reading time? Writing time? One option is to have a time of day (e.g., just after lunch) or a day of week (e.g., every Friday) specifically devoted to project-based instruction. This may allow you to sidestep, to some degree, labeling the project with a particular domain. Another option is to place it in the block that makes the most sense in terms of topic. For example, a bird guide for a local nature sanctuary might be created during science, whereas a letter to the editor about creating bike lanes might be created during social studies. Of course, to place project work in a particular content area slot, you need to make sure that it really foregrounds that discipline—otherwise the danger is that it is supplanting the important work you need to be doing in that content area.

INTEGRATED READING AND WRITING

You may be wondering what to make of the fact that project-based instruction involves reading and writing instruction within the same block of time. You may remember a time when reading, writing, and the content areas were often integrated, for example, under the auspices of thematic teaching, but today, this is the exception, not the rule in U.S. elementary classrooms. Typically, there is a time devoted to "Readers' Workshop," "Guided Reading," or "Reading" and a separate time of the day devoted to "Writers' Workshop" or "Writing." And it's not just that reading and writing are separated temporally, they are also separated conceptually. I often observe a Writers' Workshop in the afternoon that bears no clear relationship to the reading students experienced in the morning. For example, in reading time, students might be reading one genre, and in writing time, they might be writing another. In reading, there might be a lesson about chunking words to decode them, but in writing time the strategy of chunking words to encode them is not presented.

What I find most vexing about the temporal and conceptual separation of reading and writing in elementary-school schedules is that I rarely meet anyone interested in defending it. I think we all know at some level that reading and writing are reciprocal processes and that instruction is likely to be most powerful when they are treated as such. Indeed, research reveals a variety of ways in which reading and writing are integrally related (Shanahan, 2006). For example, a recent meta-analysis found that writing instruction actually improves reading (Graham & Hebert, 2011) and, not surprisingly, another found that more effective teachers have students writing more of the time (e.g., Pressley et al., 2001).

My read of the CCSS is that they lend themselves to integrating reading and writing. Consider, for example, this pair of standards from grade 1 (with emphasis added):

Reading, Standard 8: Identify *the reasons an author gives to support points in a text.*

Writing, Standard 1: Write opinion pieces in which they introduce the topic or name the book they are writing about, *state an opinion, supply a reason for the opinion,* and provide some sense of closure.

Or these pairs of standards from grade 5 (emphasis added):

Pair 1:

> **Reading, Standard 2:** Determine two or more main ideas of a text and explain how they are supported by key details; *summarize the text.*

> **Writing, Standard 8:** Recall relevant information from experiences or gather relevant information from print and digital sources; *summarize or paraphrase information in notes and finished work,* and provide a list of sources.

Pair 2:

> **Reading, Standard 6:** Analyze *multiple accounts of the same event or topic,* noting important similarities and differences in the point of view they represent.

> **Writing, Standard 7:** Conduct short research projects that use *several sources to* build knowledge through investigation of different aspects of a topic.

These close connections between reading and writing standards at the same grade level lend support to instructional approaches that integrate reading and writing—approaches such as project-based instruction.

So the fact that project-based instruction integrates reading and writing is a strength of the approach. Now, you may be required to, or just choose to, continue to devote separate parts of your day to reading and to writing, in which case your project-based time may be the one part of your day that does not have that separation. Or you may find that project-based instruction leads you to reorganize your day without separating reading and writing. Your decision should be based on the constraints and preferences of your teaching situation.

FINDING TIME FOR PROJECT-BASED INSTRUCTION

On the one hand, the press for time we all feel as educators today is very real. Students are expected to meet higher standards than ever before, there is more content to learn than ever before, there are more technological tools to use than ever before, and yet students are in school about the same amount of time as they have been for decades. On the other hand, studies reveal ineffective uses of time in many U.S. classrooms: transitions that take too long, interruptions that are unnecessary, instructional time spent on activities that research suggests do not actually work, and so on. You and your colleagues may want to start this journey toward project-based instruction for teaching informational reading and writing by looking for "time wasters" in your day—practices that, if eliminated, could help make room for project-based instruction. Debbie Miller (Miller & Moss, 2013) described one school's experience of looking for ineffective uses of time. She reported that across the grades, teachers were able to find an additional 60 to 125 minutes a day by identifying such time wasters as doing calendar-related activities for extended periods of time, morning announcements, inefficient transitions and packing up to go home, lining up in a "school-y" fashion (rather than the more time-efficient way people naturally form lines outside of school), and ineffective classroom activities (e.g., filling in worksheets).

In *No More Sharpening Pencils During Work Time and Other Time Wasters*, Elizabeth H. Brinkerhoff and Alysia D. Roehrig (2014) dove deeply into research and practical strategies for maximizing use of classroom time. This book, the Miller and Moss book cited in the previous paragraph, and books in the Not This, But That series edited by Ellin Oliver Keene and me identify widely used but ineffective classroom practices and suggest alternative practices that are more effective. I encourage you to use these and other resources to find time you can repurpose for project-based instruction.

SPECIAL WEEKS FOR PROJECT-BASED UNITS?

Some schools choose to have a week or two weeks within a year in which normal instructional routines are suspended and they focus on a project. Although this has the advantage of providing extended periods of time during the day to work on a project, and may be a good first step for schools and teachers just beginning to explore project-based instruction, I worry that it doesn't provide enough time over the course of the year for this kind of teaching. It may lead teachers and students to think of project-based instruction as "extra"—something to try to fit in around the regular curriculum. In the end, I ask you to consider how much students are actually learning in the regular curriculum versus what they are learning from the kind of teaching described in this book. I hope you will come to see project-based units as central to the school year.

How Are Project-Based Units Structured?

The unit structure I share in this book (which is certainly not the only structure one could use for project-based units) generally involves 15 to 20 sessions and approximately 45 minutes per session. (I use the term "session" rather than "lesson" because there is more going on than just lessons.) The units are made up of five major phases: the first and last phases are typically only one session each, and the middle three phases may be five to seven sessions each:

1. **Project Launch** establishes the purpose of and audience for the project.

2. **Reading and Research** mainly involves building necessary background knowledge and gathering information for the project.

3. **Writing and Research** primarily focuses on drafting the product of the project and conducting additional research as needed.

4. **Revision and Editing** involves making improvements to the product.

5. **Presentation and Celebration** involves reaching the intended audience with the product and celebrating that accomplishment.

These phases are not rigid—students will do some writing during the Reading and Research phase and some, or considerable, reading during the Writing and Research phase—but they provide a general guide. Each of these phases is described in Part 2. Within each session, we recommend a three-part structure:

- **Whole-class lessons** (10–15 minutes): The teacher provides explicit instruction about one or more teaching points aligned with the standards and related to the unit project, often reading aloud a text or text excerpt as part of this teaching.

- **Small-group, partner, and/or individual work** (25–30 minutes): The teacher provides instruction and support for needs-based small groups and/or circulates throughout the classroom coaching students as they engage in work related to the unit project.

- **Whole-class wrap-up** (about 5 minutes): The teacher pulls the class back together as a whole, reviews key instructional points from the whole-class lesson, and leads the sharing of student work as it reflects those key points.

Chapters Three, Four, Five, and Six provide details about what "goes into" each of these session components at each phase.

Why these three components with these time allocations? Regarding the whole-class lesson, research shows over and over again how valuable it is to provide explicit instruction in what we want students to learn, whether comprehension strategies, writing strategies, vocabulary, text structures, writing mechanics, or the like (e.g., Graham, McKeown, Kiuhara, & Harris, 2012; Shanahan et al., 2010). The whole-class lesson is a time to do that, as well as to use other research-supported instructional techniques, such as text-based discussion and sharing of mentor texts (e.g., Dressel, 1990; Murphy, Wilkinson, Soter, Hennessey, & Alexander, 2009).

Regarding the small-group, partner, and/or individual work, we know that students need lots of time every day to engage in reading and writing (e.g., Graham et al., 2012; Shanahan et al., 2010) with the teacher available to coach and support individually and in small groups. We want this to be our largest chunk in a session because research has revealed that one of the characteristics of more effective schools and teachers is that they have students in small groups more of the time and spend more time engaged in coaching, rather than telling (Taylor, 2011). We also want students to be engaged in cooperative or collaborative activities during this time, as a number of studies indicate that this significantly increases literacy achievement (Puzio & Colby, 2013).

Although I do not know of any research on the whole-class wrap-up, I believe it too is an essential component of unit sessions. Many students need review and reinforcement of content they have been taught in whole-class lessons, as well as opportunities to discuss how they applied it during small-group, partner, and/ or individual work time. I think of the whole-class wrap-up as allowing us to pull a thread through from the beginning of a session to the end. So, for example, if you did a lesson on ascertaining the meaning of unfamiliar words while reading, the wrap-up would be an opportunity for students to share occasions during their small-group, partner, or individual work when they came across words that were unfamiliar to them and how they tried to figure out their meanings. If you presented a lesson on how writers use graphics to persuade, you might point out in the whole-class wrap-up some particularly persuasive graphics some students are using in their writing. Whole-class wrap-up is also a great time to remind students of the purpose of and audience for their project—the reason for all their hard work.

Concluding Thoughts: Unit by Unit

Like any new endeavor, incorporating project-based learning into your classroom will initially take some preparation and patience on your part. But again, start with one unit and see how it goes. Research strongly suggests that project-based learning is an effective approach. I believe you will agree when you see how your students respond to standards-aligned lessons in the context of reading and writing with an authentic purpose and audience. Let this book guide you as you proceed, unit by unit.

CHAPTER TWO Designing Project-Based Units to Teach Informational Reading and Writing

This chapter provides an overview of the process of designing project-based units that develop informational reading and writing ability. I walk you through the Project-Based Unit Planning Template in Appendix A, so you may want to bookmark that or make a copy of it to have next to you as you read. You also may want to make a copy of the Sample Project-Based Unit Planning Sheet in Appendix B. This chapter has five major sections: Identifying Your Instructional Goals; Identifying the Genre(s) for Your Project; Identifying Your Project's Purpose, Final Product, and Audience; Planning Your Project Sessions; and Gathering Your Texts.

Identifying Your Instructional Goals

The first step in designing a unit is to think about your instructional goals. These are not the goals students will have for the project—I talk about those later in the chapter—but rather the goals that you have for the unit as a teacher. They may include:

- Building on strengths and addressing weaknesses you have observed through assessment or observation

- Having students read and write a specific genre or genres

- Addressing standards in one or more specific domains (science, social studies, mathematics)

- Addressing specific standards

- Developing specific knowledge, attitudes, and/or skills beyond those identified in the standards

- Taking advantage of specific student interests and assets (particular areas of strength or expertise)
- Capitalizing on families' interests and assets

Ideally, a unit arises from a combination of several of these goals. For example, you might have done some writing prompts at the beginning of the school year (see Chapter Five) that suggest a strong need for more instruction in teaching informative/explanatory writing. You might then have identified several specific CCSS that deal with informative/explanatory reading and writing that you want to address. You might also have noticed that the immigrant students in your class, despite your best efforts, feel marginalized in the classroom and school, so you want to develop a project that will position them as experts and change others' knowledge of and attitudes toward them. You are also cognizant of some geography standards for the grade level that you want to address.

This whole set of factors might give rise to a Country of Origin Project. In this project, each student would conduct research, write, and present an informative/explanatory text about his or her country of origin or another country of his or her choice in a gallery. The gallery would be open not only to classmates but also to other students in the school and key invited members of the community. Here is what the Project-Based Unit Planning Template would look like at this point:

Project-Based Unit Planning Template

Project Name: _____Country of Origin_____ Project Developer(s): _____Nell Duke_____ Number of Sessions: _____

Project/Students' Purpose: __Share information about a country with the local community__ Audience: __Classmates, schoolmates, community__ Final Product: __Text on a student-selected country__

Focal Genre(s): __Informative/explanatory__ Domain(s): _____ Key Standards: _____

	Text	Whole-Class Lesson	Small-Group, Partner, and Individual Work	Whole-Class Wrap-Up	Standards Addressed
Project Launch (Session 1)					
Reading and Research Phase*					
~~Session 2~~					

Identifying the Genre(s) for Your Project

One of the decisions you need to make in developing a project involves identifying the genre or genres on which you will focus. The first thing to understand is that, although a project may focus on one or more genres, "genre study" does not constitute a project. "Genre study" is a moniker for instruction in which a class spends an extended period of time, a month for example, with the focus on learning about a particular genre. Students or the teacher might say something like, "This month we're learning about how-to text." or "We're doing a unit on folktales and fables." As you might guess—and more so once you read Chapter Three—I am not enthusiastic about genre study, and the fact that you are taking the time to read this book suggests to me that you may feel the same way. My biggest concern with genre study is that instead of engaging students in reading and writing a genre for some compelling beyond-school-alone reason (as in project-based instruction), students are reading and writing to "study it," which just isn't as compelling—even to a nerd like me who *likes* to study different forms of text, let alone to an eight-year-old boy.

Another concern with genre study is that it often entails more focus on the form and features of a genre than on the purposes and strategies for reading and writing that genre. There is a place for teaching form and features, but not at the expense of learning to use the form and features to communicate.

Another reason to avoid genre study, or any genre-of-the-month approach, is articulated by Duke, Caughlan, Juzwik, and Martin (2012):

> Focusing on a single genre at a time may prevent students from understanding that genres often act within systems or genre sets (Bazerman, 2004; DeVitt, 1991; Prior, 2009). People rarely use isolated genres in everyday life but typically conduct activities within, or through, or with the mediation of systems or sets of genres. For example, in campaigning for a change in our property tax assessment to lower our property taxes, we might read a chart of current assessed and taxable values of all properties on our block on the assessor's website. We then use data from the chart as evidence as we craft a persuasive letter to the city assessor

stating why our assessed value is too high relative to those of other properties. Finally, while talking with a friend, we might tell the story of what a headache it was to change the taxable value of our home. Each of these specific genres is marshaled for the larger purpose of lowering our property taxes or sharing that experience. Each has particular features that serve the purpose of each particular communication. In real life, we combine genres to suit our purposes, moving from one to another as needed. We want students to see how genres can work together to accomplish larger purposes. Studying a genre a month too often has a myopic focus that crowds out other genres and their relationships to one another. (p. 110)

It is true that one genre may end up getting the most attention within a project. For example, a project in which students develop a book on science investigations to sell at a museum gift shop is likely to feature how-to or procedural texts above all others. However, other genres are likely to be involved. Students might read and write scientific explanations (informative/explanatory text) about why the investigations yielded the results they did, which writers commonly do in books of science investigations. Students might write letters or e-mails back and forth with the shop's manager to help arrange the sale. Students might read persuasive texts from various organizations to help them decide to which organization to donate their profits. And so on.

Take a moment to think back to the Country of Origins project. What kinds of text, other than informative/explanatory, might be read and/or written during that project?

Perhaps students would read or write nonfiction narratives of their own migration to the U.S. to include in the exhibit. Perhaps students would advertise their exhibit to the community (a persuasive text). Perhaps students would prepare a proposal to the PTO for funding to support food and drink at the gallery event (another persuasive text). In sum, a project may require the use of many genres. We need to keep our minds open to these genres even as our instructional focus may be one particular genre.

STANDARDS

In most states, the CCSS provide one guide to practice. As you may know, the CCSS contain a set of 10 standards per grade level focused specifically on Reading Informational Text (as opposed to Reading Literature). If you haven't already bookmarked those standards at http://www.corestandards.org or printed them, I encourage you to do so.

The CCSS do not have separate writing standards for literature and informational text, but text type is nonetheless evident. The first writing standard at every grade level has to do with writing persuasive text; the second writing standard at every grade level has to do with writing informative/explanatory text; and the third standard at every grade level has to do with writing narrative text (both fiction and nonfiction narrative). Some types of text named as informational text genres for the reading standards are not specifically named in the writing standards—most notably, biography and procedural, or how-to, text. Given the purposes and features of these genres, I assume biography belongs under the informative/explanatory text standard (Standard 2) or, less commonly and depending upon the subject matter and structure, the narrative standard (Standard 3). Procedural text is probably best seen as falling under informative/explanatory text (Standard 2), although that is not a perfect match. Standards 4–10 do not name specific text types; each is applicable to most or all informational genres.

In addition to the Reading Informational Text and Writing standards, Foundational Skills, Language, and Speaking and Listening standards may be addressed in project-based units for informational reading and writing. For example, Standard 3 for Foundational Skills (under "Phonics and Word Recognition") asks that students "Know and apply grade-level phonics and word analysis skills in decoding words" (and goes on to specify what those phonics and word analysis skills are for the grade level) (p. 16). Students can work on these skills while reading informational text for a project, just as they might when reading in a more traditional context. You might even focus a lesson on specific sound-letter relationships students need to learn because they occur frequently in the texts they are reading (e.g., teaching –tion prior to reading a text that repeatedly refers to our nation).

Similarly, a number of Language standards can be addressed through project-based units. For example, Standard 2 for Language forms the basis of the editing checklists I discuss and include in Chapter Six. Standard 4 for Language can figure into many units because of the vocabulary demands that many informational texts pose. Finally, consider the six anchor standards for Speaking and Listening:

Comprehension and Collaboration

1. Prepare for and participate effectively in a range of conversations and collaborations with diverse partners, building on others' ideas and expressing their own clearly and persuasively.

2. Integrate and evaluate information presented in diverse media and formats, including visually, quantitatively, and orally.

3. Evaluate a speaker's point of view, reasoning, and use of evidence and rhetoric.

Presentation of Knowledge and Ideas

4. Present information, findings, and supporting evidence such that listeners can follow the line of reasoning and the organization, development, and style are appropriate to task, purpose, and audience.

5. Make strategic use of digital media and visual displays of data to express information and enhance understanding of presentations.

6. Adapt speech to a variety of contexts and communicative tasks, demonstrating command of formal English when indicated or appropriate. (p. 22)

You can imagine how each of them—and its corresponding grade-level standard— could be addressed through project-based units involving informational text. For example, in one project colleagues and I developed, students used PowerPoint® software to present a proposal to a government official to make improvements in a local park (Halvorsen et al., 2012). Within the presentations, some classes used graphs to convey results from a survey they conducted on park improvements,

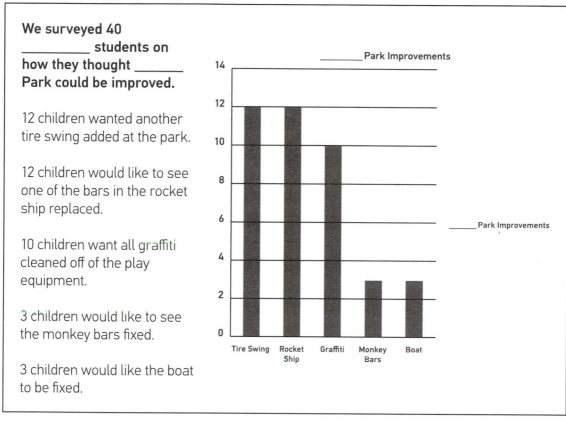

We surveyed 40 _____ students on how they thought _____ Park could be improved.

12 children wanted another tire swing added at the park.

12 children would like to see one of the bars in the rocket ship replaced.

10 children want all graffiti cleaned off of the play equipment.

3 children would like to see the monkey bars fixed.

3 children would like the boat to be fixed.

_____ Park Improvements

_____ Park Improvements

Tire Swing   Rocket Ship   Graffiti   Monkey Bars   Boat

FIGURE 2.1: Student graph showing park survey results

like the one above (the name of the school and park are blank because this was part of a research project in which confidentiality was assured).

The project helped students meet Anchor Standard 4: "Present information, findings, and supporting evidence such that listeners can follow the line of reasoning and the organization, development, and style are appropriate to task, purpose, and audience" (p. 22).

I wish that I could say that planning units and addressing CCSS is an entirely linear process, but it is not. For example, you may start with specific CCSS and perhaps also content area standards that you want to address, but as you plan the unit, you may see it is going to be difficult to address a specific standard you'd hoped to, or you may see an opportunity to address a standard you hadn't intended to address. Expect a certain amount of back-and-forth between the planning and the standards. In my view, this is just fine as long as over the course of a year, you are addressing all the standards that you are expected to address.

Of course, addressing a standard does not mean that students actually attain it. Monitoring their acquisition of specific standards should inform which standards to address and in how many projects to address them. You can use a grid to keep track of which students have shown evidence of meeting specific standards and to help you plan future units. (See pages 106–107.)

THE CRAFT OF WRITING

The CCSS are an important guide to our practice, but, as indicated earlier, our instructional goals should not be entirely limited to them. One important omission in the elementary writing standards is that they tend to focus on elements of writing but not on the quality of those elements. For example, they might ask for an introduction but say nothing about the quality of that introduction—does it grab the reader's attention, is it clear, is it well organized, and so on. For this reason, I like to supplement the elementary CCSS for writing informational text with five standards that deal more with the quality or craft of writing:

1. Grab your readers' attention from the start.

2. Be interesting. Keep your readers' attention.

3. Organize information in a way that will make sense to your readers.

4. Help your readers "see" information by using graphics.

5. Help your readers understand by making your writing clean and clear.

Obviously, this list isn't very detailed and it isn't meant to be exhaustive, but I think it offers a reasonable compromise between caring about craft and keeping planning and expectations manageable.

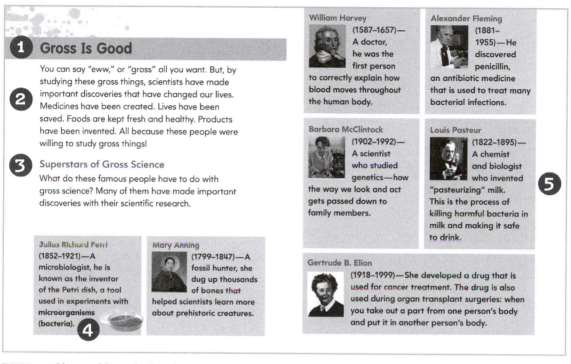

FIGURE 2.2: This spread from a book entitled *Gross Science!* (Geller, 2014) captures the five craft standards listed on page 32.

LEARNING ABOUT STUDENTS AND FAMILIES' INTERESTS AND FUNDS OF KNOWLEDGE

The elementary CCSS don't say a word about building on or developing students' interests, but doing that can be enormously helpful in getting students to the point where they can actually meet the standards. A long line of research indicates that higher interest leads to stronger performance and that instruction that deliberately focuses on student interest produces gains in achievement (e.g., Ainley, 2006; Guthrie, McRae, & Klauda, 2007). In fact, research shows that students even read at a higher reading level when what they are reading is on a topic of interest (Jiménez & Duke, 2014). Focusing so much on having students read at their identified reading level can often cause teachers to lose sight of the fact that identified reading level changes depending in part on the reader's interest. In Appendix C, I have included a survey you can use or adapt to learn about students' informational text reading and writing interests. You can use the survey results, as well as informal observations and conversations with students, to inform your instructional goals and shape projects in ways that will capitalize on students' interests. That said, one of the values of a project-based approach is that you can often create interest with a clear, compelling purpose and audience—interest that might not otherwise surface. For example, I once saw a group of fourth graders more fired up about reading and writing information books about light and sound than I could ever have imagined possible. Why? They were reading and writing those books for a group of Ugandan children who have little access to English texts. (See Duke, Caughlan, Juzwik, & Martin, 2012, for details.) Their teacher, Kathleen Jayaraman, along with fellow teacher LeAnn Thelen, at Delta Center Elementary School in Grand Ledge Community Schools, came up with the project as a way to teach a traditional topic in a more meaningful way while also building students' informational reading and writing skills.

Name: _____ Date: _____

I want to learn more about what you do and don't like to read and write. Please tell me how you really feel. It's okay if you don't like every kind of reading and writing.

What are some things you like to read and write about?

_____
_____
_____

What are some things you don't like to read and write about?

_____
_____
_____

Please circle all of the kinds of things you like to read or watch:

Fictional Picture Books	Newspapers	Comic Books
Informational Picture Books	Websites	Manga
Chapter Books	Videos	Textbooks
Encyclopedias	TV Shows	
Magazines	Dictionaries	

Understanding families' interests and expertise can also inform your instructional goals and project development. In a classic work, Moll, Amanti, Neff, and Gonzalez (1992) wrote of families' "funds of knowledge"—understandings and skills families have developed, sometimes over generations, that enable them to run their households, as well as function and thrive in their daily lives. These funds of knowledge can help expand the knowledge, skills, and experiences you can offer students, make meaningful connections between home and school, convey to students the relevance of material they are learning, and lend a greater degree of authenticity or "real worldness" to your curriculum. To continue on with the example of the light and sound unit above, perhaps part of students' research could have been to learn from a classmate's parent who is an electrician. Perhaps the family of one of your students emigrated from Indonesia and could share his or her knowledge of shadow puppetry. Perhaps students could learn more about practical applications of understanding sound from a parent who deejays on the weekend or who plays in a musical group.

One of the challenges in incorporating families' funds of knowledge is learning about what those funds are. This can be especially difficult when families have had negative experiences with schooling themselves and have been made to feel that nothing they know or can do is valued in a school context. Here are some strategies to consider for learning about families' funds of knowledge and reducing negative associations with schooling:

Conduct home visits before the start of the school year, with a major aim being to learn about some of each family's funds of knowledge. Maybe you notice a quilt hanging on the wall and learn that a member of the family is a quilter—a great resource for making real-world geometry connections. Maybe you find out that a parent is a carpenter—a great resource for any projects that involve building.

Have an informal social gathering early in the school year and explain to families that you would love to hear about their hobbies, jobs, religious or cultural traditions, and anything else that might connect to projects you'll be doing in school this year. Give specific examples so parents understand that any type of hobby, job, or tradition is appreciated.

Take a few minutes at the end of the first parent-teacher conference to learn more about how the family spends its time outside of school, making clear that your role is not to judge but to build on their child's and their family's interests and assets.

Send home a survey, if you know your families are able to read and write in English, that asks questions about their hobbies, jobs, and traditions, again making the purpose clear to reduce families' concern that you are there to judge them.

Some of the best teachers I know—including teachers from high-poverty settings— derive pleasure through the relationships they develop, and the things they learn, from families. I encourage you to make families part of your project-based instruction.

Identifying Your Project's Purpose, Final Product, and Audience

With your instructional goals in place, it is time to identify the *students'* purpose for the project, as well as the final product and the intended audience for the final product.

PURPOSE

Some people believe that a project-based unit must have a driving question. I believe that a project must have a driving purpose, which could be addressing a question, but could be something else, such as addressing a need in the local community. To identify the purpose of the project (that is, students' purpose in doing the project), I like to start by thinking about the situations *outside of school* in which people read and write the kind or kinds of text I want students to read and write. For example, I might ask myself, "In what situations do people read and write how-to or procedural text?" (Some answers: when they are building something, when they are learning how to operate something, when they are cooking, when they are carrying out procedures in a lab, and so on.) With those kinds of situations in mind, I think about a real-world problem that could be solved, a need that could be addressed, or a question that could be answered with that kind of text. For example, I might think, "Because many senior citizens in our community don't know how to operate some of the digital devices they would like to, maybe students could write directions for how to operate them." Or I might think, "Because the city's science museum has designed exhibits with investigations for visitors to carry out, maybe students could design and write procedures for how to do that."

A project's purpose can be close to home, as in those examples, or it can be far away, as in projects about ensuring adequate clean water supplies in another country, protecting endangered habitats across the globe, or teaching children elsewhere in the world about U.S. history. When coming up with a purpose, you should consider:

- Problems, needs, or questions in your school
- Problems, needs, or questions in your local community
- Problems, needs, or questions around the country or even the world
- Current events
- Your connections and resources (people you know in the community, partnerships with your school, and so on)
- Businesses and organizations in the community
- Students' interests and assets
- Families' interests and assets
- Upcoming events and opportunities

Regarding this last point, sometimes it is not a problem or need that gives rise to a project, but an opportunity. Perhaps your students have kindergarten buddies, and you see an opportunity for them to write books to read to those children. Perhaps there is a festival coming up in the community, and you see an opportunity for students to share what they're learning with people who would be interested. The most important thing is that students see the project as having a real purpose for reading, writing, and learning beyond just satisfying a school requirement.

THE FINAL PRODUCT

Once you have identified a purpose for the project, it is time to think about the final product students will create. (The final product could be a written text, such as a book or magazine, or it could be a video, an audiofile, and so on.) If, for example, the purpose of the project is to get people to make greater use of a local park in danger of being shut down for lack of use, persuasive texts make sense. And, from there, you must determine the type of persuasive text—flyers or advertisements for the park, a letter to a newspaper or local online news site, a promotional video about the park (based on a written script and storyboard), a pamphlet about the park, and so on. You may generate, as is the case here, more ideas than can be reasonably created in one project, so consider your pedagogical goals to determine one to focus on.

An important consideration in identifying the format in which students will write is to think about what already exists in the world. A trip to the local public library will reveal dozens of information books about Mexico, so having students engage in a project to write books about Mexico may not make sense. There is the danger that students will think, "Why should I work so hard on this book about Mexico when there are already books on this topic that are better than mine will be?!" A better idea might be to have students write a text that is not so readily available (e.g., a pamphlet about Mexico) or to write a text that is different in an important way from what has already been published (e.g., written for younger children than currently available books; written in a different form than currently available books—a Mexico wiki site maybe) or at a better price point than currently available texts. (The books referenced earlier, written for children in Uganda, for example, were much less expensive than existing commercially published books.)

It is so important, in identifying the final product for a project, to think about types of text that are read and written outside of school. Compare/contrast essays, reports (in the school sense of the word), or dioramas are types of text that are commonly employed in schools but are rarely used outside of school. The final product you choose to focus on may have some elements of these types of text, but they need to resemble types of text found outside of schools. For example, students might compare/contrast or have elements of a school "report" in an informational pamphlet, or they might incorporate a diorama into a larger museum-style exhibit.

Resist the temptation to keep falling back on books as a format that students write. Although I have observed many successful projects in which students produced books, I have also observed successful projects in which they produced other types of text. Consider the following the types of text:

- Pamphlets
- Brochures
- Booklets
- Magazines
- Blogs
- Guides
- Advertisements
- Flyers
- Posters
- Signs
- Commercials
- Promotional videos
- Informative or documentary videos
- Promotional websites
- Informative websites
- Letters
- E-mails

As explained earlier, a project may involve reading and writing many types of text. On the line that says "Final Product" in the planning sheet in Appendix A, fill in the specific text that addresses the project purpose, such as "Letters to the Houston Chronicle." Where it says Focal Genre(s), fill in the genre or genres in which the project's final product—and texts used to address it—fall. For example, these letters would be persuasive text, and students might read a lot of informative/explanatory text to inform their writing of that type of text.

AUDIENCE

Informational text written for a project should have an audience that is going to read, view, and/or use the text students produce for the purpose for which the text is intended. That audience will vary by genre, as shown in the following table:

TABLE 2: EXAMPLES OF GENRE, PURPOSE, AND AUDIENCE

Genre	Purpose	An authentic audience would. . .	Example	*Non*-Example
Informative/ explanatory	To convey information about the natural or social world	Want or need to know that information	Young visitors to a community receiving a "My Favorite Places" guidebook compiled by local kids	A teacher receiving an information book on a state she already knows a great deal about
Persuasive	To influence the reader's ideas or behaviors	Be potentially influence-able	A letter to the editor of the local newspaper persuading readers to honor traffic rules in a school zone	A principal receiving an essay arguing for having recess all day every day; it's not going to happen
Nonfiction narrative	To interpret and share the story of a real event	Have an interest in or relevance to the story	A middle school class learning about an event that changed the history of its community	Kindergarten buddies hearing a story of a historic event that is hard for them to grasp
Biography	To interpret and share the experiences of a real person	Have an interest in or relevance to the person	A baseball team receiving a biography of a baseball player who overcame obstacles	A classical music enthusiast receiving a biography about a teen pop star
Procedural	To teach someone how to do something	Want or need to know how to do that thing	A TV or radio presentation on how to participate in a national bird count	An adult receiving a text from a child on how to drive a car or do a risky skate trick

Why do I place such an emphasis on writing for an audience? There is both theory and research that language is learned best, perhaps only, in real communicative contexts—contexts like those that gave rise to the language or genre in the first place. For example, Victoria Purcell-Gates, Nell K. Duke, and Joseph A. Martineau (2007) studied the degree to which students had opportunities to read and write informational and procedural text in science for purposes beyond just learning to read and write science text. Students who were provided such opportunities, using more authentic texts, showed higher growth on reading and writing measures than those who were provided reading and writing opportunities and texts that were more "school-y" in nature. Several studies have shown that students produce better writing when they are writing for an audience beyond the teacher, such as an international pen pal or a best friend (Cohen & Riel, 1989; Crowhurst & Piche, 1979). Although these and other studies have been carried out with writers older than the elementary grades, a recent study with second graders confirms the value of students' writing for an audience beyond the teacher (Block, 2013). In this study, second graders wrote informative/explanatory texts alternately for their classroom teacher or for the local public librarian. Children's texts were scored by raters who did not know whether that text was written for the classroom teacher or the local public librarian. In the end, texts written for the local public librarian had higher holistic or overall scores and scored higher in focus, accuracy, details, illustrations complementing text, language of informational texts, and navigational features. I have noticed the same phenomenon in my own teaching at the college/university level: When my students are writing for their mentor teachers or for a research or practitioner journal, their writing is of higher quality than when they are writing for just me. It seems that we as classroom teachers are the worst possible audience for our students' writing. Yet another benefit of a project-based approach to instruction is that we create situations in which students are writing for an audience beyond ourselves. That said, there may be some situations in which students are writing to you for a truly compelling purpose in which you are the natural and authentic audience; for example, if students write to you about different simple machines in preparation for a forthcoming move in your family (Duke, Purcell-Gates, Hall, & Tower, 2006/2007) or if students are trying to convince you to change some aspect of the classroom or some classroom rule.

BEWARE FAKE PURPOSES AND AUDIENCES!

Sometimes educators develop projects with fake, or inauthentic, purposes and audiences. For example, one project I came across had students create a travel brochure to persuade people to take a vacation on a planet in the solar system other than Earth. Given that no audience of which I am aware is actually going to take a vacation to another planet, to whom are children actually writing and for what purpose? The audience and purpose are undermined. Another project I recently came across had third graders pretending to be particular animals and then writing letters to Santa persuading him to believe that they are the best animal to pull his sleigh and carry out other tasks for him. Given that students are not actually animals, and many of them would not expect Santa to actually read these letters in the first place, the purpose and audience are undermined. Although these kinds of projects may seem motivating—and they are likely better than writing for no purpose or audience at all—genre theory and research suggests they are not as compelling as reading and writing experiences that address a real question or solve a real problem for a real audience.

NOT JUST YOUR GRANDMA AS AUDIENCE

It's tempting to make the audience for students' projects Grandma, Mom and Dad, and others close to children. Although this is fine some of the time, don't overdo it. Children probably realize, on some level, that they don't have to work as hard or cater as deliberately to a familiar audience—Grandma is likely to be pleased with pretty much whatever they do. Furthermore, generally speaking, the stakes are lower. Whether or not Grandma is pleased may not have the kinds of consequences as, for example, whether the mayor is compelled by the students' proposal or whether the wildlife commissioner is impressed enough by students' qualifications for them to participate in a national bird and butterfly count. And as a familiar audience, Grandma does not help us address the CCSS, which ask that students ". . . learn to appreciate that a key purpose of writing is to communicate clearly to an external, sometimes unfamiliar audience, and they begin to adapt the form and content of their writing to accomplish a particular task and purpose" (p. 18). Not only does this exclude Grandma, but it also excludes classmates and even schoolmates, who would be considered an internal, if not familiar, audience. Again the consideration here is that we want to identify audiences for whom students will do their best writing.

Planning Your Project Sessions

Having determined the purpose, final product, and audience for your project, it is time to plan the project sessions. In this part of the process, the most challenging task, in my experience, is making sure you don't get so swept up in getting the project done that you overlook the specific standards and content you need to address. Indeed, sometimes instruction will slow down the progress of a project somewhat. For example, one of your goals for a project may be teaching students strategies for ascertaining the meaning of unfamiliar words they encounter when reading. Instruction in these strategies is important. It can help students with the reading and research they do on the project's topic, and can even help inform their writing (e.g., by providing awareness of and strategies for giving readers clues to the meaning of unfamiliar words and phrases). But the instruction alone will not do much to move the project along. Students aren't likely to produce a lot of notes, sentences, or paragraphs by the end of a session that immediately contribute to the project. This is fine—the material being taught is important and it does serve the project. (If you have something to teach that really doesn't serve the project, it should be taught in another context.) It is a constant balancing act to both maintain project momentum and provide the rigorous instruction students need.

You will notice that the planning sheet in Appendix A is divided into five sections. These cover the five phases of a project briefly described in Chapter One:

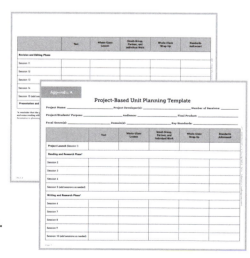

- Project Launch

- Reading and Research

- Writing and Research

- Revision and Editing

- Presentation and Celebration

In the sections that follow, I provide more detailed commentary about each of these phases.

PROJECT LAUNCH

The launch of a project is when students learn of the purpose, text, and audience for the project. Typically, the launch occurs in just one session, as is reflected on the planning sheet in Appendix A. Usually, but not always, it is the first session of the unit. One of the chief goals of the launch is to get kids excited about the project—to engage and motivate them, pique their curiosity, build wonder—as well as, in most cases, establish the purpose and audience. Sometimes, the launch consists of sharing a request from an outside source, as in, "Friends, Principal Johnson has asked us for a big favor. He would like us to be in charge of writing an informative/explanatory pamphlet about the school for Curriculum Night." Other times, the launch comes from the students. Other times, the launch is partly teacher-generated, partly student-generated. For example, you might share an e-mail from a friend saying she wishes there was a book that tells people how to make some of the crafts she sees kids making nowadays, such as rubber-band bracelets and origami cups. Students are likely to respond by suggesting they write such a book. Or you might bring in an article about homelessness in the community and see what kinds of responses unfold and what project that suggests.

Some advocates of project-based learning would say that all projects should come from students. I do not agree with this position. I do think it is important for students to "buy into" the project (see Chapter Three, pages 62–63), but I do not believe every project, or perhaps even most projects, need to come from students. Projects that are planned by teachers in advance have many advantages, including the opportunity for more time to prepare the project and ensure it aligns to standards and other instructional goals. Some of the studies reviewed in Chapter One—in which project-based instruction led to improvements in learning and/or affect—were projects that did not come from students. Such projects can nonetheless offer lots of room for student input. For example, one of the projects in the Halvorsen et al. (2012) study involved students in visiting a local park, identifying deficiencies in the park, and writing a proposal to a local government official to make improvements to it. I have observed this unit being implemented in multiple school systems. Because the parks vary, the deficiencies students choose to focus on vary, and their authorial choices vary, I have found that each classroom makes this unit to some degree its own. This is part of why I believe it can work for teachers to collaborate and share units (see Chapter Eight)—units can still be shaped by student input.

READING AND RESEARCH

In the Reading and Research phase of a project, students mainly build necessary background knowledge and gather information for the project. They listen to and/or read a variety of texts—written, visual, and oral. For example, if students are developing a promotional video about a local nonprofit medical clinic, they might read about the clinic, take a field trip to the clinic, read informative/explanatory texts about the kinds of work done there, interview the staff, and so on.

It is important to note that we call this phase reading AND research, not just reading. This is because research can involve lots of data gathering that require skills other than reading, as illustrated in the previous paragraph. For more about that, see the section on Source Texts later in this chapter. The number of sessions in this phase of a project may vary; Appendix A has listed four, with encouragement to add more as needed.

WRITING AND RESEARCH

During the Writing and Research phase, students begin composing what will eventually be the final product of the project. They engage in planning the text, for example, using a graphic organizer or specific strategy they have been taught. And they actually draft or compose the text. Planning and drafting are two vital steps in the writing process. (See box, pages 47–48.) The steps can occur on paper but, at least some of the time, should occur with digital tools. This not only addresses the Common Core State Standards, but also reflects research, which actually shows that the use of word processing software improves weaker readers'/writers' writing quality, length, development/organization, writing mechanics, and writing motivation (Morphy & Graham, 2012, a meta-analysis).

Notice that this phase is not just called the "Writing" phase but the "Writing and Research" phase. This is because when writers are planning and drafting, the need for additional research often surfaces. You probably experienced this when writing in college or preparing a report or other document in your professional life. It's the reason that I like to talk about the "Research Sandwich"—the concept that steps in the writing process may be sandwiched by research when the writer is composing informational text. We might start by conducting research, do some planning, realize in the course of the planning that we need to conduct additional research, begin drafting, then see again the need for additional research, and, in some cases, even conduct research during the Revision and Editing phase in response to feedback or questions about the writing. This is one reason why the number of sessions in this phase of a project may vary. The planning sheet in Appendix A provides space for five sessions but with encouragement to add more as needed.

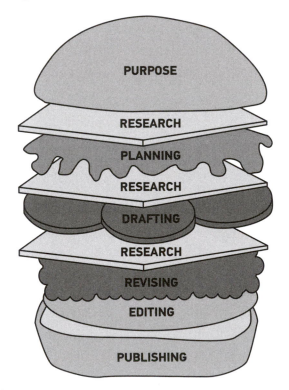

FIGURE 2.3: The "research sandwich"

THE WRITING PROCESS: RESEARCH AND PRACTICE

The What Works Clearinghouse Practice Guide *Teaching Elementary School Students to Be Effective Writers* (Graham et al., 2012) gives the recommendation to "teach students to use the writing process for a variety of purposes" a rare "strong evidence" rating (pp. 12–13), meaning that there are many rigorous studies supporting the efficacy of this approach (although as noted earlier, the approach has little impact on motivation or on the writing of struggling students [Graham & Sandmel, 2011]). The guide describes the writing process as follows:

> The writing process is the means through which a writer composes text. Writing is not a linear process, like following a recipe to bake a cake. It is flexible; writers should learn to move easily back and forth between components of the writing process, often altering their plans and revising their text along the way. Components of the writing process include planning, drafting, sharing, evaluating, revising, and editing. An additional component, publishing, may be included to develop and share a final product.
>
> **Planning** often involves developing goals and generating ideas; gathering information from reading, prior knowledge, and discussions with others; and organizing ideas for writing based on the purpose of the text. . . . Students should write down these goals and ideas so that they can refer to and modify them throughout the writing process. [Planning occurs during the Reading and Research and Writing and Research phases of the project structure I have presented in this book.]
>
> **Drafting** focuses on creating a preliminary version of a text. When drafting, students must select the words and construct the sentences that most accurately convey their ideas, and then transcribe those words and sentences into written language. Skills such as spelling, handwriting, and capitalization and punctuation also are important when drafting, but these skills should not be the focus of students' effort at this stage . . . [Drafting occurs during the Reading and Research and Writing and Research phases of the project structure I have presented in this book.]
>
> **Sharing** ideas or drafts with teachers, other adults, and peers throughout the writing process enables students to obtain feedback and suggestions for improving their writing. [Sharing occurs during the Revision and Editing phase of the project structure I have presented in this book.]

Evaluating can be carried out by individual writers as they reread all or part of their text and carefully consider whether they are meeting their original writing goals. Evaluation also can be conducted by teachers and peers who provide the writer with feedback. [Evaluating occurs during the Revision and Editing phase of the project structure I have presented in this book.]

Revising and editing require that writers make changes to their text based on evaluations of their writing. Revising involves making content changes after students first have evaluated problems within their text that obscure their intended meaning. Students should make changes to clarify or enhance their meaning. These changes may include reorganizing their ideas, adding or removing whole sections of text, and refining their word choice and sentence structure. [Revising occurs during the Revision and Editing phase of the project structure I have presented in this book.]

Editing involves making changes to ensure that a text correctly adheres to the conventions of written English. Students should be particularly concerned with reviewing their spelling and grammar and making any necessary corrections. Editing changes make a text readable for external audiences and can make the writer's intended meaning clearer. [Editing occurs during the Revision and Editing phase of the project structure I have presented in this book.]

Publishing typically occurs at the end of the writing process, as student produce a final product that is shared publicly in written form, oral form, or both. Not all student writing needs to be published, but students should be given opportunities to publish their writing and celebrate their accomplishments . . . [Publishing occurs during the Presentation and Celebration phase of the project structure I have presented in this book.] (p. 14)

As you see, I view the first two components of the process described—planning and drafting—as occurring during the Writing and Research phase of projects (though planning, and even some early drafting, may begin during the Reading and Research phase). I view the next four components—sharing, evaluating, revising, and editing—as occurring during the Revision and Editing phase of projects. The final component—publishing—I see as occurring during the Presentation and Celebration phase of projects.

REVISION AND EDITING

The fourth phase of a project-based unit is Revision and Editing. In my experience, elementary writing instruction tends to break down along these lines:

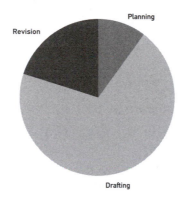

FIGURE 2.4 Typical breakdown of elementary writing instruction

I believe it should often look more like this, at least when it comes to writing informational text:

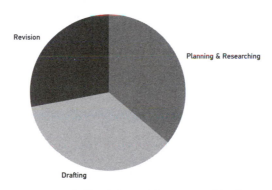

FIGURE 2.5 Recommended breakdown of elementary writing instruction

Why? First, I think that spending the vast majority of time on drafting does not reflect the reality of writing informational text for many adult writers (certainly if this book is any indication!), who spend considerable time researching, planning, and revising. Second, there is a lot of research on the value of teaching revision and editing, as well as planning writing, particularly for struggling writers (Graham et al., 2012). Third, the CCSS set a high bar for revising and editing, with a standard on revision at each elementary grade level, for example:

Grade K, Standard 5: With guidance and support from adults, respond to questions and suggestions from peers and add details to strengthen writing as needed.

Grade 5, Standard 5: With guidance and support from peers and adults, develop and strengthen writing as needed by planning, revising, editing, rewriting, or trying a new approach. (Editing for conventions should demonstrate command of Language standards 1–3 up to and including grade 5 on pages 28 and 29.)

I do believe that becoming a great writer has much more to do with becoming a great reviser than many people realize. An Internet search on revision allows you to read a lot of commentary from professional writers about revision, perhaps the most graphic being Raymond Chandler's, "Throw up into your typewriter every morning. Clean up every noon."

You may be groaning as you read this—not just because of Chandler's quotation but also because you find that it is hard to get children to revise. "I'm done" is such a familiar chorus. The good news is that we have reason to think that students are more inclined to revise when they are writing for a real purpose, as in project-based instruction.

> "Writing without revising is the literary equivalent of waltzing gaily out of the house in your underwear."
>
> —Patricia Fuller

The Block (2013) study I mentioned earlier indeed found that students made more mechanical revisions and more content revisions when writing for a specified purpose than when writing for an unspecified purpose. This fits with what I have seen and heard anecdotally: Teachers who have tried project-based instruction have told me that they have never seen their students work harder on their writing or spend as much time on revision and editing. As you'll read in Chapter Six, I also recommend a structured approach to revision and editing that may help students engage in it differently than what you may have experienced in the past.

Presentation and Celebration

The final phase of project-based units is Presentation and Celebration. In this phase, the final product of the project is delivered to its audience. For example, if students wrote guides to an aquarium, they might visit the aquarium to hand out the guides to visitors and leave copies for future visitors. Or if going to the aquarium is not possible, students might ceremoniously pack up their guides (keeping a set of copies for themselves) to be mailed to a representative from the aquarium, or that representative might visit the classroom to receive the guides.

It is essential to project-based instruction that the product reach its intended audience (and, if at all possible, that that audience responds to it—see Chapter Seven). I often tell teachers and administrators that in the Presentation phase you fulfill your contract with students for the project. If you don't follow through, if you don't actually get the final product to its intended audience, it can undermine students' "buy in" for future projects you or others might offer.

Celebrating the completion and delivery of the project is also important. I recommend tightly linking celebrations to the project itself. For example, if the project is a blog about your state for potential visitors, the celebration might involve eating foods that come from your state. For more examples of celebrations tightly linked to project foci, see Chapter Seven.

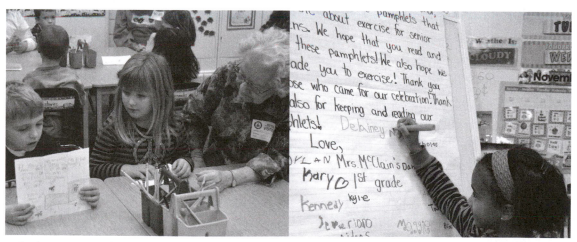

Students wrote pamphlets persuading senior citizens to exercise. They celebrated by inviting senior citizens to their classroom and then sending the pamphlets to a local senior residence.

Gathering Your Texts

In a project-based approach to teaching informational reading and writing, you can think about a "text trifecta." There are three kinds of texts used in projects:

1. Launch Texts

2. Source Texts

3. Mentor Texts

LAUNCH TEXTS

Launch texts are read aloud to the class at the start of a unit. They are used to help inspire students about the project and build their enthusiasm for and background knowledge about the topic. With regard to the launch text, it is important to remember how many scholars think about "text"—it can be written, visual, oral, and combinations thereof.

The launch text could be a letter from the director of a local botanical garden asking students to create guidebooks for the garden. It could be a video documenting the deplorable living conditions in a particular part of the world that students could work to help. The launch text could be an online article about a figure in the local community that you encourage the class to publish a biography about. The launch text could be a visit from the activities coordinator of a local senior living facility talking about some of the needs and interests of the residents there (a possible audience for subsequent reading and writing). Or, of course, the launch text could be an actual children's book. Consider, for example, Page McBrier's picture book *Beatrice's Goat* (2001), a true story of how a child's life changed after her family's receipt of an animal from Heifer Project International, a charitable organization that donates livestock to poor communities around the world. This book might be used to launch a unit that involves raising money (through persuasive text) and awareness (through nonfiction narrative and/or informative/explanatory text) about the charity.

Source Texts

Students gather information for their project from source texts—informative/explanatory websites, magazine articles, books, encyclopedias, photographs, informational videos, and so on.

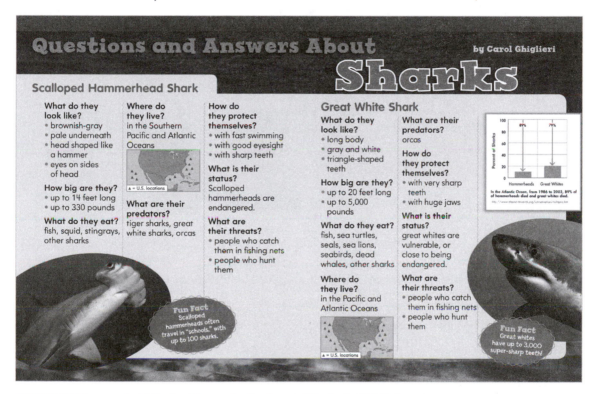

FIGURE 2.6: This source text tells about hammerhead and great white sharks (Ghiglieri, 2014).

Some source texts may be developed, in a sense, by students themselves, as when they conduct interviews or administer and analyze surveys to gather information for the project. Source texts may also help students with the process of research. For example, a text on how to interview or how to design a survey could operate as a source text for students.

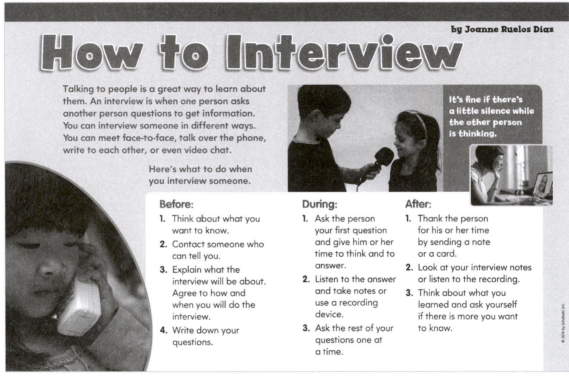

How to Interview

by Joanne Ruelos Diaz

Talking to people is a great way to learn about them. An interview is when one person asks another person questions to get information. You can interview someone in different ways. You can meet face-to-face, talk over the phone, write to each other, or even video chat.

It's fine if there's a little silence while the other person is thinking.

Here's what to do when you interview someone.

Before:
1. Think about what you want to know.
2. Contact someone who can tell you.
3. Explain what the interview will be about. Agree to how and when you will do the interview.
4. Write down your questions.

During:
1. Ask the person your first question and give him or her time to think and to answer.
2. Listen to the answer and take notes or use a recording device.
3. Ask the rest of your questions one at a time.

After:
1. Thank the person for his or her time by sending a note or a card.
2. Look at your interview notes or listen to the recording.
3. Think about what you learned and ask yourself if there is more you want to know.

© 2014 by Scholastic Inc.

FIGURE 2.7: This source text helps students plan and conduct an interview (Diaz, 2014).

Finding source texts appropriate for students' reading levels can be one of the greatest challenges teachers face. There is no easy answer to this, but here are some tips:

Don't get too worked up about level. As indicated earlier, students can read at a higher level when they are interested in the topic. Having relevant background knowledge also helps, a point underscored by Timothy Shanahan (2014).

Think about scaffolding. There are ways to make normally inaccessible texts accessible for students. (See Chapter Four.)

Remember that not all source texts have to be written (although some should). Photographs and recordings of interviews can operate as source texts. Videos can operate as source texts as well. Research by Lauren Fingeret (2008) and other researchers has demonstrated that young children can learn important material from video.

Consider rewriting texts to students' reading levels. This is not as difficult as you may think, and can greatly increase the range of sources available for students.

Make extensive use of the web. There are many online sources of information for children that are deliberately written for beginning reading levels, such as http://ngexplorer.cengage.com/ngyoungexplorer/ and http://classroommagazines. scholastic.com.

Engage librarians. At many public libraries, you can call about a particular topic and librarians will gather resources on it in advance of your visit. You can specify approximate reading level. Of course, a school librarian, if you have one, can be a valuable resource as well.

A final consideration about source texts: Make sure they aren't so close to the final product in terms of content, format, and text type that students are tempted to plagiarize or to wonder why their own text is needed in the first place.

MENTOR TEXTS

The third kind of text in the text trifecta I recommend are mentor texts. A mentor text serves as a model, or mentor, for students' own final product. Mentor texts should match the type of text students are writing themselves and should include features and craft that you want to teach during the unit.

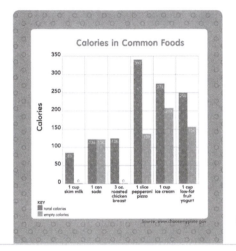

As mentioned earlier, it takes about 1,500 calories to power the average 6-year-old for one day. It's important to choose those calories wisely. This graph shows the number of empty calories in some common foods. Can you spot the healthiest foods?

Calories in Common Foods

KEY
total calories
empty calories

Source: www.choosemyplate.gov

11

Eat for Your Heart

Want a healthy heart? Then eat right! Eating lots of fatty and salty foods is bad for your heart. And it can lead to being overweight. Heart disease is a serious problem, making many Americans sick every year. To keep your heart healthy, eat a balanced diet made up of fruits and vegetables that are the colors of the rainbow, whole grains, nuts, fish, chicken, and low-fat dairy products.

Fatty deposits on an unhealthy heart

12

FIGURE 2.8: These pages are from a book—Eat Right to Be Your Best (Carson, 2014)—that might be used as a mentor text for teaching students about how graphics are often used to persuade.

Although the genre and features of a mentor text should match what students are writing, the topic and content of the text generally should not. If the mentor text addresses the same topic and content students are addressing, there is a danger that students will imitate that text too much—or even plagiarize. Again, the existence of the text might undermine their own purpose for writing. They might ask, "Why do I need to write this text when there is a perfectly good one our teacher has just read to us?" It can be useful, however, if the topic and content of the mentor text are *related* to what students are writing.

Mentor texts do not have to be perfect. It can be useful to talk about ways students would like to improve upon them in their own writing. (For an instructional technique related to this, see Chapter Four, pages 101–102.) In fact, sometimes I value using anti-mentor texts: Poorly structured informative/explanatory texts can help students better understand the need for structure, insufficiently specific steps in procedural text can help students better understand the need for specificity, and so on.

Mentor texts also do not have to be chosen by you. They can be chosen by students, using questions to guide them. For example, fifth-grade teacher Niki McGuire of Greenwood Elementary School in Grand Ledge, Michigan, engaged students in critiquing a set of potential mentor texts by asking questions such as:

- What do you like about the way this book presents the information?
- Is there anything you think would make the book better?

Students then decided among themselves which text would be used as a mentor text. (For discussion of how to use mentor texts, see Chapter Five.)

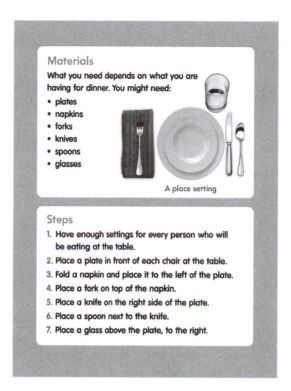

Materials

What you need depends on what you are having for dinner. You might need:
- plates
- napkins
- forks
- knives
- spoons
- glasses

A place setting

Steps
1. Have enough settings for every person who will be eating at the table.
2. Place a plate in front of each chair at the table.
3. Fold a napkin and place it to the left of the plate.
4. Place a fork on top of the napkin.
5. Place a knife on the right side of the plate.
6. Place a spoon next to the knife.
7. Place a glass above the plate, to the right.

FIGURE 2.9: This text—How to Do Chores at Home (Weinberger, 2014)—might be used as a mentor text for teaching students a structure for procedural writing.

Concluding Thoughts: You're Up!

At this point, you have all the basics you need to design a project-based unit to support informational reading and writing development, using the planning sheet in Appendix A. Appendix B provides a sample unit from Grade 5 to further your understanding. I have given many workshops in which I have shared much less information and fewer examples with the audience than you have at this point, and I have seen some excellent projects come out of them. So don't be shy about trying your hand at designing a project right now! Chapters Three through Seven focus on project phases and will therefore deepen your knowledge about designing and implementing units. They will be important to read as you move forward in this work. Chapter Eight provides advice about making project-based instruction more manageable by being strategic in designing projects for a given school year, sharing units, and collaborating with colleagues.

CHAPTER THREE
The Project Launch

The project launch is the single most important phase for conveying the purpose, product, and audience for a project to students. The project launch phase and launch texts are described in Chapter Two, pages 44–45 and 52. In this chapter, I share tips for a successful launch, examples of launch sessions, and some strategies you can use at the launch, as well as throughout the unit, to manage whole-class and small-group, partner, and individual work time.

Tips for a Successful Launch

Below are some tips for a successful launch. I encourage you to add notes to the margins with other tips you come up with in your early experiences with project-based instruction.

Decide on the audience. Before launching a project, you should know what the audience for a project is going to be, or at least what the audience options are for students to choose among or how you will guide students in researching and deciding on an audience themselves. If you know who the audience is going to be, it is important to contact potential audience members and make sure they are interested in being involved in the project. You should be clear about whatever that involvement entails, such as making texts available to museum patrons or using placemats that children have created for customers in a restaurant. You should ask audience members whether they would be willing to send a response or convey responses to students about their near-finished and finished work. Responses are so important (for reasons explained in Chapter Seven) that if it is not clear the audience members will be willing to send them, you may want to rethink the audience.

Choose your launch text carefully. The launch text or texts need to inspire students, build necessary background knowledge, and be accessible to students. To figure out what might inspire students, put yourself in their little shoes: What would they find compelling? To figure out what background knowledge they need, have a brief conversation in advance of the session with a few students in the class to find out what they know about the project's particular topic, key vocabulary, or concepts. Chances are, you have lots of practice assessing texts for their student accessibility. Use it. For example, you may have to revise some potential launch texts so they will be sufficiently accessible to students. Perhaps you elicited a letter from a local businessperson to launch a unit on how to make money, but that well-meaning adult wrote a letter that you know will be way over your students' heads. You may need to make some revisions to the letter, or read it aloud with some brief explanations of word meaning, so it serves its purpose as a high-quality launch text.

Convey your excitement through language and gesture. I once had the pleasure of observing a kindergarten teacher, Tara Kras of Jayno Adams Elementary School in Waterford, Michigan, as she informed her students that they would be writing reminder notes (this was part of a project to create informative/explanatory posters on reasons people write; one of the reasons students studied was writing to remember). Tara leaned way in to students, she used a quiet tone, she spoke at a pace that built suspense, and she used language that conveyed enthusiasm—something like, "Friends, I have some very exciting news for you. Today, we are going to get to write our very own reminder notes!" Children gasped, mouths and eyes open wide. Some of the children looked positively frozen in excitement. Mind you, these were just reminder notes—"No gym Friday," "Ask Shantae to come over," and so forth—and yet students were mesmerized. Tara created this excitement through language and gesture. Of course, I am not suggesting that you rely on enthusiasm alone to launch a project, but it certainly helps.

In *Early Intervention for Reading Difficulties*, a book on a research-tested approach to early literacy instruction (which, by the way, I highly recommend), Donna M. Scanlon, Kimberly L. Anderson, and Joan M. Sweeney (2010, p. 61) provide a compelling look at more and less motivating ways to communicate with students:

TABLE 3: COMMUNICATION WITH STUDENTS

Unmotivating messages	Motivating messages
"We need to read this book today before recess."	"We get to read this book today before recess."
"I want to see what you are going to write next. You need to finish your journal entry before you to go the block area."	"I can't wait to see what you are going to write next. I hope you get to finish your journal entry before you go to the block area."
"Let's see how many of these letters you know."	"Let's see how many of these letters you *already* know."
"Each of you will do a report on dinosaurs."	"You will each have a chance to do a report on a dinosaur that you are especially interested in."

Note. From *Early Intervention for Reading Difficulties: The Interactive Strategies Approach* (p. 61), by D.M. Scanlon, K. L. Anderson, and J. M. Sweeney, 2010. New York: The Guilford Press. Copyright, 2010 by the Guilford Press. Reprinted with permission.

Assess the launch. It is important to double check to make sure your launch results in students being able to identify a purpose, final product, and audience for the project. A great way to assess this is to enlist an adult who wasn't in the room during the initial launch to walk around the classroom, asking students about the project. Do students correctly explain the project? The final product? The audience? In fact, throughout a unit it can be helpful for other adults to ask students, "Why are you writing that?" or "Why are you reading that?" If the answer comes back, "Because Ms. Jones told me to" or "Because it's writing time," that's a good indication that the launch did not quite work, and should be re-approached or perhaps the project should be shifted altogether. (See the next section for more on this.) Instead, you want exchanges like these:

> **Q:** Why are you reading that?
>
> **A:** I'm trying to learn more about seals, so I can help people understand why they shouldn't kill them for their fur.

> **Q:** Why are you reading that?
>
> **A:** I want to see how this author used diagrams because I want to put some diagrams in my proposal to save a local ecosystem.

Q: Why are you writing that?

A: The students at Johnson School don't have any books about force and motion, so we are writing these books for them.

Q: Why are you writing that?

A: Mr. Walker has termites in his house, so he wants us to teach him about them.

Be ready to shift your plans. It is so important to make sure students "buy into" the project and to be ready to shift your plans if they do not. My favorite anecdote about this comes from kindergarten teachers Patty Koutoulas and Lisa Thompson of Mitchell Elementary School in Ann Arbor, Michigan. Their students had clearly been hearing and seeing a lot at home about Hurricane Sandy, and so Lisa and Patty wanted to do a project that had something to do with the disaster. The idea, which I am guilty of suggesting in the first place, was to engage students in raising money for the victims of Hurricane Sandy—"Nickels for New Jersey" or something along those lines. Specifically, the idea was that students could generate persuasive texts—oral, drawn, and written—to try to convince others to donate money to this cause. When they presented the idea to students, however, there was little interest. Students were not compelled by this purpose. In retrospect, I should have seen this coming from an experience with my own son when he was around kindergarten age. I told him in detail about the typical North American tooth fairy tradition. (See Selby Beeler's *Throw Your Tooth on the Roof* [1998], an information book about how other traditions deal with lost teeth.) He listened intently and then, after pausing for a few moments said, "You mean they want me to give up a *real human tooth* just for some money?!" Lisa and Patty, to their credit, did not push forward with their idea, as I think some teachers would. Instead, they shifted course mid-launch and listened to students talk about what they would like to do and how they would like to help. Their students gravitated toward more relational ideas. In particular, they expressed the feeling that the children affected by Hurricane Sandy must be scared, and they, too, have been scared at times. Eventually, students landed on the idea of sending children stories about a time they were scared and what they did to feel better. They also made worry dolls out of clothespins and sent those, along with a how-to text about how to make them, to a school in New York that had many children who were affected by the hurricane. This anecdote is important for us to keep in mind as we think about the project launch. We need to be ready to be somewhat flexible and adjust projects as needed to get students to "buy in." (And don't worry—Lisa and Patty made sure to address persuasive text in another project-based unit.)

Don't let perfect be the enemy of good. It may be that no matter how hard you try, not every student buys into the project, particularly if you have a student with narrow interests ("I only like trains!"), a student with oppositional defiant disorder, or a student who might be so turned off of school that it is hard to get him or her engaged in anything that happens there. What can you do in such cases?

- Give yourself permission to fully engage most children with most projects, but not every single child with every single project. The reality is that even if half of your students are compelled by the project's purpose, final product, and audience, that is a lot more than are likely to be compelled by many forms of traditional instruction.

- Consider giving each hard-to-inspire student a special role in the project to increase his or her engagement. For example, a student who is only interested in computers could become your "technology guru," helping classmates use digital tools for publishing. Or perhaps a student could be responsible for corresponding with the intended audience for the project.

- Consider creating a mini-project for the student. For example, if he or she is not interested in writing persuasive texts to convince people to save a downtown landmark, perhaps you could ask the student whether instead he or she would like to write an argument to the school board about why members should vote to invest more money in digital devices for the district.

- Finally, be thinking about that student and the next project you offer—perhaps you can think of one that is more likely to be a hit with him or her.

Have an activity that will support the launch. A launch session should not be made up of only whole-class time, in which you read the launch text to students and discuss the project, but rather it should also include some small-group, partner, or individual work. Perhaps after the whole-class reading and discussion, you disperse students to take notes on what they know about the audience for the project. Perhaps you ask students to write letters to family members introducing the project they will be working on and requesting donations of materials that will support it. Perhaps you have students draw or write letters introducing themselves to audience members and alerting them to what is to come. For example, in one project, first graders drew pictures of themselves engaged in their favorite form of exercise to introduce themselves to a group of senior citizens to whom they would later be sending pamphlets about the importance of exercise.

Consider wrapping up with a visual. Recall that the third recommended component of each session is the wrap-up, in which you pull the class back together, review key instructional points from the whole-class lesson, and lead a sharing of student work that shows evidence of learning. The launch session's wrap-up should first and foremost summarize the project, final product, and audience. You might consider creating an anchor chart like the one below that lists these three elements, perhaps with a representative picture next to each one, especially for kindergartners and first graders.

Examples of Launch Sessions

Following are two examples of launch sessions using the three-part structure I described in Chapter One:

- **Whole-class lessons** (about 10–15 minutes): The teacher provides explicit instruction about one or more teaching points aligned with the standards and related to the unit project, and often reads a text or text excerpt as part of the lesson.

- **Small-group, partner, and/or individual work** (about 25–30 minutes): The teacher provides instruction and support for needs-based small groups and/or circulates throughout the classroom coaching students as they engage in work related to the unit project.

- **Whole-class wrap-up** (about 5 minutes): The teacher pulls the class back together as a whole, reviews key instructional points from the whole-class lesson, and leads the sharing of student work as it relates to those key points.

The purpose, final product, and audience for the units from which these sample sessions come are given below. Session plans follow on pages 66 and 67.

TABLE 4: PURPOSE, FINAL PRODUCT, AND AUDIENCE FOR SAMPLE UNITS

Project Title	Purpose	Final Product	Audience
Reducing and Reusing Messages	To persuade shoppers or diners in the community to reduce and reuse	Placemats or paper bags with messages about reducing and reusing	Restaurant or grocery store customers
Protect Our "Pests" Posters and Leaflets	To persuade schoolmates to think differently about creepy creatures	Posters and accompanying leaflets about the benefits of so-called "pests."	Schoolmates

LESSON 1: Project Launch for Reducing and Reusing Messages

Whole-Class Lesson

- Read aloud Launch Text. Discuss terms *recycle*, *reduce*, *reuse*. Ask questions about key details: *Why did this community decide to recycle, reduce, reuse? How did they do it? What difference did it make? How do recycling, reducing and reusing help our world? How can we help our world? What do you wonder about recycling, reducing, and reusing?*

- Launch project: Tell students that they can help our world too! They can help get more people to reduce and reuse. Explain that they get to draw and write messages about reducing and reusing on grocery bags that will be used at a real grocery store! Describe business. Say something like this:

  Country Market is a grocery store in town. It sells goods such as fresh vegetables, canned goods, paper towels, and cleaning supplies. I often go there to buy the food my family eats and supplies I need around my house. Country Market knows you're going to be working to become experts in reducing and reusing. Cashiers there load customers' goods into paper bags. Country Market has given us 25 of those paper bags. At the end of this unit, you'll be writing this message on those paper bags: your expert opinion about how important it is to reduce and reuse and how Country Market customers can do that. Then I will take the bags to Country Market, so cashiers can give them to their real customers!

- Discuss idea of audience: *Whenever we are writing, we want to think who our audience is, or who will be reading what we write. When we write messages on the grocery bags, who is our audience?*

- Show photos of Country Market, and its newspaper ads, and project its website. Talk about what students notice. Ask what else students know about the market.

- Tell students they will get to draw and write about the project audience. Prompt them to think about who shops at Country Market, and why (e.g., *Firefighters buying napkins for the firehouse. Parents buying food for their children*).

Individual or Small-Group Work Time

- Have students draw and write about project audience (e.g., *Firefighters buy napkins for the firehouse.*)

Extra support: Pull together a small group to work on generating ideas about audience beyond examples discussed in Whole Class, forming legible letters and drawing pictures.

Extra challenge: Extend writing about audience, including a profile of a shopper and his or her purpose.

Dual Language Learners: Make videos and photographs with labels and captions about reducing, reusing, and recycling available to help students deepen their knowledge and connect words to concepts.

Whole-Class Wrap-Up

Discuss and display student work. Refer to it throughout the unit and remind students of purpose and audience.

FIGURE 3.1: Session plan to launch a kindergarten project on reducing and reusing messages

Students Will:

- Answer questions about key details in Launch Text (value of reducing, reusing, and recycling).

- Learn about the project: creating messages for paper bags that encourage shoppers to reduce and reuse.

- Think and write about the project's audience: shoppers at Country Market.

Standards:

RI.K.1 With prompting and support, ask and answer questions about key details in a text.

W.K.7 Participate in shared research and writing projects (e.g., explore a number of books by a favorite author and express opinions about them).

Materials:

- Launch Text, *Kids Help the Earth*

- writing and drawing supplies

LESSON 1: Project Launch for Protect Our "Pests" Posters and Leaflets

Whole-Class Lesson

- Ask students to name animals or insects they think are "disgusting."
- Read aloud Launch Text. During reading, ask, *Where do bees do much of their work? How do woodpeckers help the environment? Why do mole tunnels help grass grow?* After reading, ask, *What is the text's main idea?* Discuss responses.
- Display the Information on So-Called "Pests" chart. Read first entry, "Honeybee," and, and, as a class, fill in the two columns, using information from the Launch Text. Do the same for the second entry, "Mayfly."

Information on So-Called "Pests"		
Animal	**How People Feel About It**	**Reason It is Beneficial**
Honeybee	Afraid of being stung	Fertilize plants; beeswax, honey
Mayfly		
Woodpecker		
Mole		

Small-Group or Partner Work Time

- Distribute copies of the chart to students and have them work in groups or pairs to fill in the third and fourth entries, "Woodpecker" and "Mole," with information they recall from the Launch Text.

Extra Support: Guide students to return to text to help them complete chart.

Extra Challenge: Have students expand information from text with their own ideas about "pests."

Dual Language Learners: Put labels written in students' home language(s) on the so-called "pests" in the Launch Text and copies of the chart.

Whole-Class Wrap-Up

- Gather students in a circle, with their filled-in charts. Ask volunteers to share what they wrote and point out places in the Launch Text from which information came.
- Launch project: Tell students they will be creating posters to persuade, or convince, schoolmates to protect so-called "pests." They will also create accompanying leaflets that contain information about benefits of those pests and why it's important to project them.

Students Will:

- Listen to and identify main idea and key details in Launch Text (importance of some animal "pests").
- Complete a chart about responses to "pests" and their benefits.
- Learn about the project and audience: creating posters with leaflets to persuade schoolmates to think differently about animal "pests."

Standards:

RI.3.1 Ask and answer questions to demonstrate understanding of a text, referring explicitly to the text as the basis for the answers.

RI.3.2 Determine the main idea of a text; recount the key details and explain how they support the main idea.

Materials:

- Launch Text, *Don't Let These Pests Bug You!*
- Information on So-Called "Pests" chart
- copies of the Information on So-Called "Pests" chart for students

FIGURE 3.2: Session plan to launch a third-grade project on protecting our "pests" posters and leaflets

BEYOND THE LAUNCH: WHEN YOU'RE IN ORBIT

We can't afford to identify a purpose, final product, and audience in the launch session and then leave it at that. We need to revisit them throughout the unit, particularly for young children, who may not have this information in the front of their minds from one day to the next. Here are some examples of how you can refer to the purpose, product, and audience in different parts of a session:

Whole-class lesson: During this time, use language in your instruction in a way that reminds students of the purpose, final product, and audience. For example, you might say:

> "Today we get to keep working on our . . . for . . ."

> "Friends, I got an e-mail yesterday from . . . They are really excited about the . . . you are writing/making."

> "I was thinking last night about . . . and how much they are going to like our . . ."

> "Yesterday at the . . . I saw a great example of a . . . like what we are writing. Take a look at this . . ."

Small-group, partner, or individual time: During this time, you can provide feedback in a way that reminds students of the purpose, final product, or audience. For example, you might say:

> "I like the detail you gave in your explanation here. I think that will really help the preschoolers understand what you're saying."

> "Right here, I'm not sure what you mean. I think you will need to make this a bit clearer for the people at the Rotary Club."

> "This is such a good example of a how-to text that really makes me want to do the procedure!"

Whole-class wrap-up: You can also remind students of the project's purpose, final product, and audience during whole-class wrap-up. You can make a statement such as, "I saw you all working really hard today to make sure the information you are including in your books is accurate. This will be great, because we don't want to give children at the Boys and Girls Club books that contain incorrect information." Or you can bring in some new information related to the purpose, product, or audience for students to think about between this session and the next. For example, you could tell students that you have learned that children at the Boys and Girls Club prefer books with pictures, so they could think overnight about how they could add more photographs or illustrations to their books.

However you choose to do it, be sure students have the project's purpose, final product, and audience in mind throughout the unit.

Strategies for Managing Whole-Class Instruction and Small-Group, Partner, and Individual Work Time

The launch session is your first opportunity in the unit to engage students in a whole-class lesson; small-group, partner, and/or individual work; and whole-class wrap-up. For project-based instruction to go well, you need to manage these components effectively. It is beyond the scope of this book to go into detail about general classroom management. (I recommend books on Responsive Classroom, a research-tested approach to classroom management, and/or a recent book Ellin Keene and I edited: *No More Taking Away Recess and Other Problematic Discipline Practices* by Gianna Cassetta and Brook Sawyer.) But I will share a few of the management practices that seem especially well-suited to whole-class and to small-group, partner, or individual instruction.

MANAGING WHOLE-CLASS INSTRUCTION

Read aloud with expression. In a pre-service course I taught recently, one of the interns wrote that a student wouldn't be expected to demonstrate good prosody (intonation, inflection, emphasis, and so on) because she was reading an informational text. This is a misconception. Informational texts, like storybooks, should be read aloud in an engaging fashion, with attention to punctuation, sentence structure, and the natural rhythms of language, and even with emphasis as appropriate (e.g., when reading that an ant can carry 10 to 50 times its own body weight!).

Use good discussion practices. At a minimum, this means:

Asking meaty questions. Such questions require higher-order thinking, extended answers, and perhaps more than one right answer, such as, "What do you think is the most important thing we learned from this text?"

Encouraging students to build on one another's responses. Rather than teacher-student-teacher-student exchanges, promote exchanges that have a higher proportion of student talk: teacher-student-student-student-teacher . . . and so on.

Asking follow-up questions. You can encourage students to support their claims with evidence from the text (an emphasis in the CCSS) and elaborate on their language and thinking by asking questions such as: "What makes you say that?" "What did we read that supports that?" or "Can you explain a bit more?"

Synthesizing. "I heard Juan, Rios, and Mariana saying that . . . Does anyone have a different view?"

Encouraging students to ask questions. CCSS K–3 Standard 3 under Speaking and Listening deals with being able to ask questions of a speaker. Ellin Keene (2012) writes also about the value of using silence in responding to children's talk. I find this so difficult (as my own children will attest!), but Keene points out that silence or wait time "gives students an opportunity to think about concepts" and "serve[s] as a model for taking time to think" (p. 870).

Encourage turn and talk. The length of whole-class lessons and wrap-up generally does not permit enough time for everyone to speak or share his or her work. Turn and talk is a great way to give students more opportunity to speak as well as to develop their ability to listen. Typically, turn and talk is done in pairs. The teacher gives students a clear topic and then students turn to face one another and discuss it. If students are not familiar with turn and talk, it is a good idea to explain to them how to take turns speaking, listening, asking questions, and making themselves understood. Role playing good and not-so-good examples of turn and talk may also be helpful.

Consider investing in a set of clipboards or dry-erase boards. These writing surfaces provide another way for students to engage actively during whole-class time. Students might use them to take notes on the text you are reading (especially if it is a source text) or points you are making (for example, features they might want to include in their writing). They can use these tools to practice contributions or additions they might make to a text the class is writing together. (See Chapter Five.) You can also use them for "Every Pupil Responds" techniques, such as asking students to write on their boards the author's opinion and hold it up, or asking them to weigh in on something, such as a topic they would like to nominate for inclusion in the project.

Gamify. There has been a lot of buzz lately about "gamification"—making material into a game. There are a lot of ways this can go awry, but when it's done well, it's a good way to break up the routine of whole-class instruction once in a while. For example, to help younger students hear the sounds within words (phonemic segmentation) in order to write them, you might make a game out of trying to stretch the longest word for the writing they'll do, or with older students you might make a game out of generating words with the same prefixes or suffixes they noticed in a source text they just read, and then discuss the meaning of those words.

SMALL-GROUP, PARTNER, AND INDIVIDUAL WORK TIME

For many teachers, small-group, partner, and individual work time presents many more challenges for management than whole-group time. In fact, I've encountered teachers who avoid it all together. But we know from research that that is not in students' best interest. Here are some tips that may help to support you in managing small-group, partner, and individual work time effectively. In addition to the books cited on page 69, *No More Sharpening Pencils During Work Time and Other Time Wasters* by Elizabeth H. Brinkerhoff and Alysia D. Roehrig (2014) may be useful to you.

Buy an ounce of prevention. You can prevent a lot of problems during small-group, partner, and individual time by making sure students are crystal clear about what to do before you conclude whole-class time. Explaining and modeling what students need to do are, of course, essential, but you may also want to write the steps on chart paper or project them, and/or have students repeat the steps with you, holding up a finger for each step, before going to work. The time this takes may save time in the long run.

Explicitly teach students how to work with partners and in small groups. Depending on where you teach, you may be the first teacher who has ever asked students to engage in partner or small-group work (especially if you are a kindergarten or first-grade teacher). Even young children can do this kind of work effectively, but they aren't born knowing how to do it. Some will do it more or less naturally due to some combination of their past experiences and their temperament. Others will struggle all the time or only sometimes with certain classmates and not with others. You will need to actually teach students how to work together. Stephanie Harvey and Harvey Daniels' (2009) book *Comprehension and Collaboration: Inquiry Circles in Action* includes a number of lessons for helping students work effectively in groups.

Halt the hand-raising. On a number of occasions, I have witnessed children working on their own with their hand raised for much, even all, of the work time. And it was painful to watch because they were unable to write, hold a book, or do much of anything productive. Develop a system for students to let you know they need help without raising their hand. One option is to give each student a question card or question block to set out on the corner of the desk when he or she has a question for you. You can keep an eye out for students' question cards or blocks, and while they are waiting for you, students can continue working on other aspects of the project or just sit quietly and read or write something else (because we want eyes on print, pen on paper as much as possible). In addition, you might consider designating, on a rotating basis, Question Captains whose job it is to know just what to do and how to do it so they can answer classmate questions as needed. (It may be helpful to meet with those Captains in advance of the session so they are clear about how to answer possible questions.)

Invoke a village. No matter how many good management techniques you put in place, project-based instruction is likely to go more smoothly if you have people helping you. You might enlist parent volunteers, retired teachers or senior citizens, Dual Language Learner (DLL) teachers, or others in the school community to help out during project-based instruction. You might form a partnership with a local business that can provide volunteers to support you. (Doing a project involving that business is a great way to start the relationship.) Or you might call on local volunteer organizations to provide support. In my experience, many volunteers welcome the opportunity to be involved in project-based units because they can relate to the project's "real world" nature. And they can appreciate the level of engagement they see in students.

Concluding Thoughts: Love the Launch

The project launch is my favorite phase of a project-based unit to think about. I love the challenge of coming up with a compelling purpose, final product, and audience and thinking about how to get students on board. The time spent meeting this challenge is well worth it as the launch is so crucial to the success of the entire project. I hope the tips in this chapter are helpful to you, leading you to love the launch, too.

CHAPTER FOUR The Reading and Research Phase

The Reading and Research phase often takes as much or more time than any other phase of a project for good reason: It is the most central for developing informational reading skills and makes important contributions to students' informational writing. I could easily write an entire book—and more—on it. As I have only one chapter, my aim is to provide basic information about when to teach, what to teach, and how to teach in the Reading and Research phase.

When to Teach the Reading and Research Phase

The simple answer to when to teach reading and research is "during every project." With a skimpy or nonexistent Reading and Research phase, we risk sending students the wrong message about informational writing—for example, that it is okay to write informative/explanatory text without building a strong knowledge base on the topic. We risk telling students that it is okay to write a persuasive text off the top of their heads, without basing their argument on data and other forms of information. So often we hear the mantra that students should "write what they know." That may be true for many kinds of literary writing, but for informational writing, authors often do a great deal of research to know more. Students should, too.

Neglecting the Reading and Research phase also means missing opportunities to build content knowledge. I can't stress enough how important content knowledge is to overall reading success. For a dramatic illustration of this, let's go back in time to 1988. In a study published by Donna R. Recht and Lauren Leslie, a group of seventh- and eighth-grade students who were either good readers or poor readers and who had either high or low knowledge of baseball were asked to read a passage describing half an inning of a baseball game. Students were then asked to reenact and summarize what they read. The researchers found a significant effect for high versus low knowledge, but no effect for reading ability. Baseball knowledge, not reading ability, predicted students' comprehension. Poor readers with high knowledge of baseball outperformed good readers with low knowledge of baseball. In fact, even when good readers had high knowledge of baseball, they did no better on the post-reading tasks than poor readers with high knowledge of baseball. Knowledge matters to comprehension. It matters a lot. Building knowledge is an essential component of effective comprehension instruction (Duke, Pearson, Strachan, & Billman, 2011).

Finally, when we neglect the Reading and Research phase, we miss an opportunity to build reading and research skills—and to do so in a manner intertwined with writing and driven by a compelling project. Most of the remainder of this chapter focuses on this aspect of the Reading and Research phase. But first, here are two general notes about supporting informational reading development.

THE PROJECT—AND BEYOND: EYES ON TEXT

By emphasizing the importance of the Reading and Research phase of a project, I don't want to imply that this is the only place in the school day in which students should be reading or conducting research with informational text. You should provide opportunities for students to read informational text during science, social studies, language arts, and other times in the day, whether you're carrying out a project or not. Recreational reading of informational text should also be promoted heavily. We want students' eyes on text, including informational text, as much as possible not only during instructional time, but also during scaffolded independent reading time in school (see Miller & Moss, 2013, regarding the importance and implementation of *scaffolded* independent reading). We also want students' eyes on text, including informational text, as much as possible outside of school. Home-based summer reading programs are effective in improving the reading achievement of children of low SES (Kim & Quinn, 2013), and there are many strategies that schools and teachers can use to make informational texts part of students' summer reading mix (Cahill, Horvath, McGill-Franzen, & Allington, 2013).

THE WRITTEN WORD—AND BEYOND: THE OCTOPUS APPROACH

Just reading written words is not enough to meet the demands of the 21st century, nor the CCSS. The ability to read graphics, video, and quantitative information is key.

Being able to learn through oral texts (e.g., presentations, interviews) is also critical. I have borrowed the term "the octopus approach" from informational text author Stephen R. Swinburne, as quoted in Laura Robb's *Nonfiction Writing From the Inside Out* (2004). The many arms of Swinburne's research process include not only reading a variety of texts on- and off-line, but also interviewing, conversing with experts and other informants, and conducting observations. We want students to develop a multi-armed approach to research—and to have the skills necessary to do that.

What to Teach in the Reading and Research Phase

At its heart, the Reading and Research phase is about texts—texts students locate, evaluate, skim, read, synthesize, and apply to the project. To support this work, students need specific knowledge and specific skills—or targets of instruction. In this section, I identify that knowledge and those skills and then share some information about texts themselves.

Targets of instruction for the Reading and Research phase are abundant and varied. In this section, I discuss seven to consider:

1. Standards

2. Use of Comprehension Strategies

3. Identification and Use of Text Structure(s)

4. Use of Graphics

5. Use of Text Features (Other Than Text Structure and Graphics)

6. Vocabulary

7. Sourcing and Evaluation

There are other targets of instruction to consider. For example, units can be an opportunity to teach decoding skills—maybe a project on thunderstorms provides an opportunity to review the th- digraph or to teach compound words. However, the seven targets listed above are among the most important specifically for informational text comprehension. Later in the chapter, I turn to how to teach these targets.

STANDARDS

For many teachers in the U.S., the primary targets of instruction in the Reading and Research phase lie in the Common Core State Standards for their grade level.

TABLE 5: MOST RELEVANT CCSS IN THE READING AND RESEARCH PHASE

Reading Standards for Informational Text K–5	All standards
Speaking and Listening K–5	• Standards 1–3 • Standards 4–6 are better addressed in the Writing and Research Phase
Language Standards K–5	• Standards 1–3 are better addressed in the Writing and Research Phase • Standards 4–6

USE OF COMPREHENSION STRATEGIES

Research strongly indicates that explicitly teaching comprehension strategies can improve students' reading comprehension. The What Works Clearinghouse, an initiative of the U.S. Department of Education, convened a panel on improving comprehension in kindergarten through grade 3. This panel was comprised of researchers (including me) and practitioners. Part of the panel members' work was to review research literature using strict criteria, generate recommendations for practice, and then give each recommendation a rating—strong, moderate, or minimal—for the strength of the evidence supporting that rating. The panel gave teaching reading comprehension strategies a rare "strong" rating for the strength of the evidence (Shanahan et al., 2010).

For most informational texts, I suggest teaching the use of the following strategies over the course of the elementary grades, recognizing that not all strategies will apply to all informational texts or reading situations:

Previewing: briefly looking over the text to obtain information about its content and structure (This should not be confused with the "picture walk," which does not appear to improve comprehension [Dougherty Stahl, 2008].)

Searching: looking for specific information in a text (With printed texts, searching may involve using the index, table of contents, and headings; with digital texts, it may involve using icons, menu bars, a search box, and so on.)

Skimming: looking or reading through text quickly and superficially, usually for the purpose of gaining a general sense of the text or looking for specific information to read more carefully

Monitoring, clarifying, and fixing up: attending to one's meaning construction and using strategies, such as rereading or asking questions, as needed if/when meaning breaks down

Activating and applying prior knowledge: thinking about what one knows related to the text (Good readers integrate new knowledge and prior knowledge while reading informational text.)

Inferring: using information in the text and prior knowledge to figure out something important to constructing meaning that is not explicitly stated in the text (*The text says . . . I know . . . and so . . .*)

Self-questioning: asking oneself questions related to the text as one reads (Questions about why or how pieces of information in a text relate may be especially helpful.)

Visualizing: forming mental pictures of text content, such as an animal behavior or the inner workings of a machine

Visually representing: using physical tools, such as Venn diagrams or reenactment, to organize and/or remember information from a text

Highlighting and annotating: using marks and notes, in print or digitally, to draw attention to particular information or responses to it

Gisting and summarizing: noting and stating the main point(s) of what is read (Good readers engage in this process while reading informational text, not only when they're finished.)

COMPREHENSION STRATEGIES AS A MEANS TO AN END, NOT AN END UNTO THEMSELVES

Notice that I titled this section "Use of Comprehension Strategies" rather than "Comprehension Strategies." I did this to emphasize that the value of comprehension strategies lies in using them to better comprehend what one is reading and, in project-based instruction, to put comprehension to use to serve a compelling purpose. In reality, it does not matter whether a student can name, describe, or even apply a comprehension strategy if that strategy does not actually result in better understanding of the text at hand and future texts he or she reads. As Ellin Keene (2008) asserts, "We want kids to use comprehension strategies if these tools serve to deepen their understanding" (p. 122).

Too often, though, comprehension strategies are taught not as a means to an end, but as an end unto themselves. For example, one classroom activity I have observed involves having students complete a worksheet by filling in what they visualized while reading for each of the five senses (that is, what they saw, heard, touched, tasted, and smelled as they read). As I watched students completing this worksheet, my own sense was that they were much more concerned with completing the worksheet than they were with understanding what they had read. I asked myself whether I, in fact, visualize with all five of my senses when I read, and my response was that I typically do not. Although I can almost taste the juicy peach when I read Roald Dahl's *James and the Giant Peach* (1961), I can't say that I recall thinking of taste at all when reading Brian Selznick's *The Invention of Hugo Cabret* (2007). I don't think this means I did not comprehend well. Indeed, a great question for you to continually ask yourself is, "Do I do this when I read?" If the answer is no, chances are it's not worth teaching your students to do it when they read.

Some of these strategies, such as inferring and summarizing, are named in the CCSS. Although others are not, they can, research suggests, contribute to Anchor Standard 10 for Reading: "Read and comprehend complex literary and informational texts independently and proficiently" (p. 10). In addition to these strategies, there are some that are useful specifically for comprehending particular types of informational text. See the section "Use of Text Features (Other Than Text Structure and Graphics)" on pages 84–90 for more about that. And there are strategies and practices that are specific to, or at least more common to, particular disciplines (e.g., Moje, 2008;

Shanahan, Shanahan, & Misischia, 2011). For example, discerning whether a text is a primary or secondary source is important to historical reading, but generally not to reading in other disciplines. Researchers and teachers are still working out which discipline-specific strategies should be taught in grades K to 5. Until they reach a conclusion, I suggest appealing to the CCSS and the content area standards relevant to a given unit to inform your thinking.

You have probably found, or will find, that some of your students will use many or all of the strategies listed in this section quite naturally, whereas other students will need your instruction. Fortunately, research is clear that strategy instruction is valuable for students who may be struggling with reading or learning in general (e.g., Gersten, Fuchs, Williams, & Baker, 2001). For a discussion of how to teach comprehension strategies, see "How to Teach in the Reading and Research Phase" on pages 98–109.

IDENTIFICATION AND USE OF TEXT STRUCTURE(S)

Another important target of instruction in the Reading and Research phase is identification and use of text structures. Some people confuse text structure with genre, but they are not the same. The text structure is how the text is organized, whereas the genre is related more to the purpose of the text. A given genre (e.g., informative/explanatory) has one clear purpose (e.g., to convey information about the natural or social world), but could have many different text structures. The CCSS name some specific text structures, for example asking that by the end of fourth grade, students "Describe the overall structure (e.g., chronology, comparison, cause/effect, problem/solution) of events, ideas, concepts, or information in a text or part of a text." A list of text structures from the What Works Clearinghouse panel described earlier appears on the next page (Shanahan et al., 2010).

Of course, a text can be organized around more than one of these structures. For example, it might describe a particular invention; then relay, sequentially, its origin; and then compare and contrast it with another invention; and so on. In addition, a text may be organized around a structure that is not listed in the chart, such as

TABLE 6: TEXT STRUCTURES

Structure	Description	Example	Common Clue Words	Sample Activities
Description	What something looks, feels. smells, sounds, or tastes like, or is composed of	Characteristics of a hurricane		Have students use the details in a descriptive paragraph to construct an illustration or three dimensional display.
Sequence	When or in what order things happen	A storm becomes a hurricane	first, then, next, after, later, finally	Assign each student to represent one event in a sequence. Ask the class to line up in order and starting at the front of the line, to explain or enact their respective events in turn.
Problem and Solution	What went wrong and how it was or could be fixed	Hurricane Katrina destroyed homes and stores, so groups like the Red Cross had to bring food and medicine from other parts of the US	because, in order to, so that, trouble, if, problem	Provide opportunities for students to act out key phases of a passage.
Cause and Effect	How one event leads to another	What happened to the people who lived in Louisiana after Hurricane Katrina	because, therefore, cause, effect, so	Have students match up pictures representing "causes" and "effects" in a game-like activity.
Compare and Contrast	How things are alike and different	How hurricanes are the same as or different from tornadoes	both, alike, unalike, but, however, than	Set out overlapping hula hoops, one to represent each side of the comparison, and have students sort visual representations of each characteristic into the shared and different areas of each hoop.

Note. From *Improving Reading Comprehension in Kindergarten Through 3rd Grade: A Practice Guide* (p. 20), by T. Shanahan, K. Callison, C. Carriere, N. K. Duke, P. D. Pearson, C. Schatschneider, and J. Torgesen, 2010, Washington, D.C: National Center for Education and Evaluation and Regional Assistance, Institute of Education Sciences, U.S. Department of Education.

this chapter, which is organized around a "When, What, How" structure. It is in part for these reasons that members of the What Works Clearinghouse panel made this recommendation about instruction in grades K to 3: "Teach students to identify and use the text's organizational structure to comprehend, learn, and remember content." In other words, teach students to figure out how a given text is structured, rather than simply memorize some common text structures. The panel gave this recommendation a "moderate" evidence rating, which might surprise some people. Text structure instruction is indeed for younger as well as older students, and certainly if you teach grades 4 or 5, text structure should be one focus of your instruction.

Use of Graphics

Using graphics in text is also an important target for instruction. Colleagues and I could easily write an entire book on this subject, but here are some key points:

- Graphics are increasingly prevalent in the texts we read (e.g., Carney & Levin, 2002).

- Standards documents and standardized tests expect students to be able to "read" graphics; for example, CCSS Anchor Standard 7 for Reading asks students to "Integrate and evaluate content presented in diverse media and formats, including visually and quantitatively, as well as in words" (p. 10).

- In an analysis of informative/explanatory texts appropriate for second and third graders, Lauren Fingeret (2012) found that 60% of the 12,238 graphics examined contained information not in the written words.

- Research by Nell K. Duke et al. (2013) found that even by the end of third grade, some students did not understand that they could glean information from graphics that is not in the written text, or that some information in graphics is more important than other information.

- That same study found that within any given grade level, pre-K to grade three, children varied tremendously in their understanding of graphics.

As such, graphics should be an important focus for instruction, and for some students more than others. Broadly, students need to understand that:

- Authors and illustrators choose and/or create graphics to achieve specific purposes.

- Graphics in informational texts are often photographs or realistic illustrations.

This may take some getting used to for students whose primary experiences have been with storybooks containing fantastical or whimsical illustrations.

- Graphics, and any accompanying labels or captions, should not be skipped while reading because they can deepen students' understanding of the written text or even provide additional information not in the written text.

Beyond those broad understandings, there are specific graphical devices with which elementary students should become familiar. The table below identifies some graphical devices commonly found in informative/explanatory text.

TABLE 7: GRAPHICAL DEVICES WITH DEFINITIONS

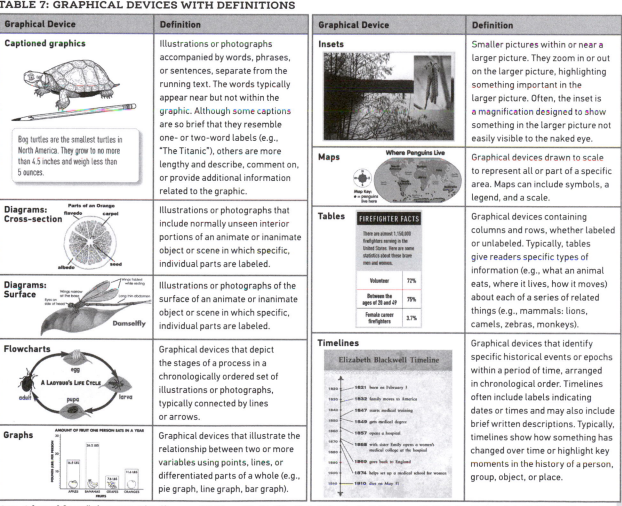

Graphical Device	Definition
Captioned graphics	Illustrations or photographs accompanied by words, phrases, or sentences, separate from the running text. The words typically appear near but not within the graphic. Although some captions are so brief that they resemble one- or two-word labels (e.g., "The Titanic"), others are more lengthy and describe, comment on, or provide additional information related to the graphic.
Diagrams: Cross-section	Illustrations or photographs that include normally unseen interior portions of an animate or inanimate object or scene in which specific, individual parts are labeled.
Diagrams: Surface	Illustrations or photographs of the surface of an animate or inanimate object or scene in which specific, individual parts are labeled.
Flowcharts	Graphical devices that depict the stages of a process in a chronologically ordered set of illustrations or photographs, typically connected by lines or arrows.
Graphs	Graphical devices that illustrate the relationship between two or more variables using points, lines, or differentiated parts of a whole (e.g., pie graph, line graph, bar graph).

Graphical Device	Definition
Insets	Smaller pictures within or near a larger picture. They zoom in or out on the larger picture, highlighting something important in the larger picture. Often, the inset is a magnification designed to show something in the larger picture not easily visible to the naked eye.
Maps	Graphical devices drawn to scale to represent all or part of a specific area. Maps can include symbols, a legend, and a scale.
Tables	Graphical devices containing columns and rows, whether labeled or unlabeled. Typically, tables give readers specific types of information (e.g., what an animal eats, where it lives, how it moves) about each of a series of related things (e.g., mammals: lions, camels, zebras, monkeys).
Timelines	Graphical devices that identify specific historical events or epochs within a period of time, arranged in chronological order. Timelines often include labels indicating dates or times and may also include brief written descriptions. Typically, timelines show how something has changed over time or highlight key moments in the history of a person, group, object, or place.

Note. Adapted from "Diagrams, Timelines, and Tables—Oh, My!" by K. L. Roberts, R. R. Norman, N. K. Duke, P. Morsink, N. M. Martin, and J. A. Knight, 2013, The Reading Teacher, 61, pp. 16–18. Copyright 2013 by the International Reading Association. Reprinted with permission. For image credits, see page 2.

I recommend that you and your colleagues come to some agreement about the graphical devices that will be taught at each grade level, with the goal of developing a common language for those devices.

Given the complexity of these graphical devices and the importance of comprehending them, I wish I could tell you that I go on to offer lots of research-tested approaches to teaching them in the elementary years, but unfortunately, research in this area is sorely needed. The broader instructional principles I present later in this chapter, however, are likely to apply to teaching graphics. For further discussion of teaching graphics, see Roberts et al. (2013) and the "More to Explore" section within that article (p. 23).

USE OF TEXT FEATURES (OTHER THAN TEXT STRUCTURE AND GRAPHICS)

Beyond text structure (and graphics, discussed in the previous section), there are many other features of informational text that may be worthy of instruction depending upon your students' needs. Again, some of these features are named in the CCSS, such as "index" in the standards for grade 2, whereas others are not. Teaching text features in isolation may not be effective (Purcell-Gates, Duke, & Martineau, 2007). I believe it makes the most sense to focus instruction on how to use the feature to improve comprehension.

Using informative/explanatory text features

Once again, the purpose of informative/explanatory text is to convey information about the natural or social world. Teaching the use of comprehension strategies and text structures supports students in learning from informative/explanatory text. Additionally, it may be helpful to teach students the following strategies:

- Paying special attention to the opening statement or general classification in a text (for example, "Crocodiles and alligators are types of reptiles.")

- Paying special attention to a general statement about or the concluding statement of a text (for example, "There are many differences between crocodiles and alligators, but they are both amazing animals!")

- Understanding the generic nature of things in informative/explanatory text (For example, when the text says "dogs" or even "a dog," it's typically referring to all dogs, not just to a particular dog, as in a storybook, or just to the dog or dogs in an illustration.)

- Understanding the universal nature of time in informative/explanatory text (For example, when the text says something like "Ants live in large groups," it means they do so all the time, not just at a particular moment in time as is typically the case in a story.)

- Making use of the very precise language typically found in informational text (for example, "White rhinos weigh 4,000–6,000 lb [1,800–2,700 kg]" rather than "White rhinos are heavy")

- Using text features, such as table of contents, index, page numbers, headings and subheadings, menus, icons, and search boxes, to pinpoint information they seek

- Making sense of special sections including prefaces, preludes, afterwards, addendums, bibliographies, authors' notes, about the author, and recommendations for future reading

(This list was informed by discourse analysis of informative/explanatory texts conducted by Victoria Purcell-Gates, Nell K. Duke, and Joseph A. Martineau [2007] and Christine C. Pappas [2006].)

Again, the focus of instruction should always be on using these strategies in order to learn from text and for compelling purposes. I don't want to see any "Identify the Addendum" worksheets, which don't offer any compelling purposes for students to learn from text!

Using persuasive text features

In writing persuasive text, the author's purpose is to influence the reader's ideas or behaviors. In a sense, then, the reader's purpose is to decide whether or not to be influenced—whether or not to accept the author's argument, to change or maintain ideas or behaviors. Depending on the grade level, it may be helpful to teach students the following strategies:

- Identifying the author's opinion or argument (opinion is the term used in the CCSS in K–5, argument and claim in grades 6–12)
  - » The introduction is often where this is first presented.
  - » Sometimes authors use a problem-solution structure, identifying the problem and then arguing for a particular solution.
- Looking for and evaluating reasons the author gives to support the opinion.
- Looking for evidence the author gives to support the reasons.
  - » The author may use numbers, graphics, and/or words as evidence.
  - » Readers should evaluate and weigh the reasons and evidence—does it help to change their ideas or behaviors?
- Looking for how the reasons are linked to the opinion, and the evidence is linked to the reasons.
- Thinking about how qualified the author is to offer the opinion, reasons, and evidence (see "Sourcing and Evaluation" on pages 91–93).
- Being aware of strategies the author may be using to persuade, such as:
  - » direct address (e.g., you, your)
  - » questions for the reader/listener ("Have you ever smelled the too-sweet, rotten odor coming from that factory?")
  - » periodic restatement of the claim
  - » attempts to establish solidarity with the audience (e.g., we, us, our)
  - » attempts to establish distance from the opposition (e.g., they, them, those)
  - » transitions that signal opposition (e.g., but, however, instead, on the contrary)
  - » logical links (e.g., because)
  - » qualifiers (e.g., often, usually, sometimes)

> » pictures or realistic photographs designed to evoke an emotional response (Duke, Caughlan, Juzwik, & Martin, 2012, p. 150)

- Looking for counterarguments or rebuttals. This strategy is not addressed in the CCSS until grade 7, but somewhat younger students can and often do want to present counterarguments and rebuttals. In writing, colleagues and I introduce the heuristic "Some people say . . . but . . ." as in "Some people say bicyclists can use the sidewalk, but that could put pedestrians at risk."

- Paying special attention to the conclusion, in which the author may restate the opinion or argument and/or discuss its importance.

(This list was informed by the original Toulmin [1958] model, the writing of Samantha Caughlan in Duke, Caughlan, Juzwik, and Martin [2012], and the CCSS themselves.)

Using nonfiction narrative and biographical text features

Recall that the purpose of nonfiction narrative is to interpret and share the story of a real event and that the purpose of a biography is to interpret and share the experiences of a real person. To help students comprehend nonfiction narratives and biographies, teach them these strategies:

- Identifying the person or people centrally involved from the beginning when teaching biography.

- Looking for indications about the degree to which the information presented is true (as opposed to fictionalized), such as:

  > » Photos

  > » Artifacts

  > » Sources/references

  > » Direct quotations

  > » Author's note(s)

- Learning about the context(s) or settings(s) in which the story or experiences occur.

- Looking for information or clues about the timing and sequence of events.

- Using descriptions in the text to envision the story or experiences (Langer, 1995).

- Identifying events or experiences in the story and clues as to why the author thinks they are important.

- Identifying problem(s) or obstacle(s) the person or people faced and how, if applicable, the problem(s) was (were) resolved.

- Looking for the theme(s) or lesson(s) of the story or experiences: Why does the author think this story or these experiences matter? Why should we? (Juzwik, 2009).

Some teachers teach "beginning, middle, and end" for reading or writing nonfiction narratives and biographies. I advise against this. The studies I am aware of that reveal improvements in narrative comprehension or narrative writing have used story elements—characters, setting (time and place), events, problem, resolution—not beginning, middle, and end (Baumann & Bergeron, 1993; Morrow, 1984).

Using procedural text features

Recall that the purpose of procedural text is to teach someone how to do something. When students are reading procedural text during the Reading and Research phase, it should be because they are doing, or at least contemplating doing, the procedure. For students to learn how to do something from procedural text, they may need instruction on one or more of the following strategies:

- Previewing for **when** the procedure would be of use, such as to address a specific science inquiry question or to prepare a particular dish, and whether they have the time, materials, and equipment necessary to do the procedure.

- Reading for **why** the author is encouraging them to carry out this procedure. Authors of procedural text often include some persuasive language in their texts. For example, a cookbook author might write at the beginning of a recipe, "Try this tangy, kid-pleasing approach to chicken."

- Reading to gather **what** materials and/or equipment are needed to carry out the procedure. This information is often contained in a section called "Materials," "Ingredients," "What You Need," or "Packing List," depending on the type of procedural text.

> » Materials are typically listed in order of use.
>
> » The author of high-quality procedural text typically includes detailed information about the materials when those details are important to completing the procedure successfully.

- Reading words and graphics for **how** to complete the procedure, which are almost always contained in a "Steps" section.

  > » The order of the steps is often indicated with letters or numbers (and less often by terms such as *first*, *next*, and *then*). These steps must be read and followed in order, which is very different from informative/explanatory text, which is often read nonlinearly.
  >
  > » Before carrying out a step, it is often advisable to reread it for understanding; after carrying out a step, it is often advisable to pause to evaluate whether it was carried out accurately according to the words and/or graphics.
  >
  > » Written steps (rather than illustrated steps) typically contain imperative verbs, or what I call "bossy words," such as *Slice . . .* , *Dissolve . . .* , or *Tape . . . .*
  >
  > » The author of high-quality procedural text typically includes detailed information about the steps when that information is important and unlikely to be inferred by the reader.
  >
  > » In a long procedure, subheadings or other devices may be used to help readers to cluster the steps. Think LEGO® construction manuals.

- Noticing any tips or warnings that the author might provide.
- Attending carefully to the outcome, as conveyed through graphics and/or words, for example, with a scientific procedure, comparing the outcome to the expected results reported by the author.

(This list was informed by a discourse analysis of procedural texts appropriate for second and third graders in science conducted by Victoria Purcell-Gates, Nell K. Duke, and Joseph A. Martineau [2007].)

Vocabulary

Vocabulary instruction improves reading comprehension (e.g., Elleman, Lindo, Morphy, & Compton, 2009), so it makes sense to use it as a target of instruction in the Reading and Research phase of a project. When we teach vocabulary, there are many pieces to consider, including teaching students how to do the following:

- Notice when the author uses words that are unfamiliar to them and seek to learn their meanings by, for example, asking questions

- Be attuned to the meaning of specific words, including their relationships to other words and subtleties in their meaning

- Infer the possible meaning of words from context

- Use their knowledge of word parts to ascertain a word's meaning

- Use print and digital tools, such as traditional and online dictionaries, to develop word knowledge

- Explore the meaning of expressions, such as idioms

Boldface walks into a bar and sits down next to Italics.

Boldface asks, "May I buy you a drink?"

Italics answers, "I'm sorry, you're not my type."

The vocabulary demands of informative/explanatory texts tend to be somewhat different than those of fictional narrative text. In informative/explanatory text, there is likely to be quite a bit of specialized or technical vocabulary, and it is likely to be repeated a number of times (in contrast, for example, to fictional narrative text, which is likely to contain many potentially unfamiliar words that only appear once). Clues to word meaning, however, may abound, whether in the running text (e.g., "Vultures feed on carrion, the flesh or meat of a dead animal."), graphics (e.g., labels in a diagram), a gloss in the margins (common in textbooks), or the glossary. Boldfaced or italicized text often signals that a word is important and may appear in a gloss on the page or in the glossary. For more about how to teach vocabulary, see pages 103–105.

SOURCING AND EVALUATION

Sourcing and evaluation may not have come to mind as important targets of instruction for K–5 students, but they are. It's important to lay the groundwork for them in the elementary years. Sourcing means finding reliable sources of information to use for a project. Those sources may include websites, trade books, magazines, reference books or sites, videos, people to interview, surveys to administer, observations to make, and so on. In the elementary years, the teacher is likely to do much of the sourcing for students, for example, collecting printed materials for students to consult and arranging interviews with relevant people. However, you can do the following things to prepare students to source on their own:

- Help students develop a schema for the different kinds of sources they might use for any given project. (See explanation of the octopus approach on pages 75–76.)

- Explain and model how you found particular sources (e.g., "Let me show you how I found this great website for our project . . .").

- Work with the school librarian/media specialist, if you have one, or with a local librarian to teach students how to search for texts in the library. An especially good time to do this is during a project for which students have chosen different topics (so they're not all going for the same three books on Utah, for example).

- Teach students how to engage in simple online searches that require them, for example, to choose keywords, search on them, and read results. Common Sense Media has a lesson plan in which students try searching with fewer and more key words and compare the results: http://www.commonsensemedia.org/educators/lesson/the-key-to-keywords-3-5.

- Consider encouraging students to try adding the words "kids," "students," or "educational" in their searches to increase the chances of finding a website that they can read independently.

- Teach students some trustworthy, go-to websites such as:

  » Kids.gov (http://kids.usa.gov)

  » National Geographic (http://www.nationalgeographic.com, especially http://www.kids.nationalgeographic.com/kids/stories)

  » Time for Kids (http://www.timeforkids.com)

  » Scholastic Classroom Magazines (http://www.magazines.scholastic.com)

Evaluating sources wisely is as important as sourcing itself. This is particularly true for websites, which range in quality and trustworthiness more than printed materials one finds in a library or bookstore. Evaluation of sources should be a focus of instruction throughout K–12 schooling, so as an elementary educator, you should not feel that you need to take full responsibility for it. However, I do believe that students should leave elementary school:

- Recognizing that not everything on the Internet is true or can be trusted (This may seem obvious to you, but research suggests that it's not to many students.)

- Habitually evaluating potential sources for appropriateness and trustworthiness

- Having a general schema for what to look for in evaluating a potential source for appropriateness and trustworthiness

Toward that end, Shenglan Zhang and I developed and tested an approach to teaching website evaluation called WWWDOT: **W**ho wrote this? What credentials do they have? **W**hy did they write it? **W**hen was it written? **D**oes this meet my needs? How? **O**rganization of the site; **T**o-do list for the future (Zhang & Duke, 2011). In our study, fourth- and fifth-grade students were taught the WWWDOT framework in four 30-minute sessions. In the first two sessions, students were taught why they should evaluate websites and the six elements of the WWWDOT framework. In the second two sessions, students prepared for and then held a debate regarding which of a set of websites were most and least trustworthy. To prepare, they examined actual websites using a WWWDOT sheet like that below. As compared to classes randomly assigned to a control group, students who experienced these four 30-minute sessions were more aware of the importance of evaluating websites and had a better understanding of what to look for when they did. Their ultimate judgments didn't yet match those of adult experts, but important groundwork had been laid. For details about the content of the 30-minute sessions, see Zhang, Duke, and Jiménez (2011).

WWWDOT

Who wrote this? What credentials do they have?

Why did they write it?

When was it written?

Does this help meet my needs? How?

Organization of site. (You can write and/or draw.)

To-do list for the future.

FIGURE 4.1: WWWDOT sheet. Download a full-size version of these pages at http://umich.edu/~nkduke/.

Let's Talk About Text, Baby

The Reading and Research phase relies heavily on texts. In Chapter Two, I described three categories of text used in project-based units—launch texts, source texts, and mentor texts. Launch texts were discussed in depth in Chapter Three; mentor texts will be discussed in depth in Chapter Five. Here, I focus on source texts, the texts students use to build background knowledge and gather information for their project. When it comes to source texts, keep these suggestions in mind:

- **Define texts very broadly** to include not only books and articles but also videos, graphics, quantitative information, artifacts, observation notes, interview transcripts or notes, surveys, and so on. (See explanation of the octopus approach, pages 75–76.)

- **Give students the opportunity to read a number of texts on the same topic.** This is explicitly called for in the CCSS document and is necessary for meeting a number of specific CCSS. These standards aside, reading many texts on the same topic can foster knowledge building and important thinking skills, such as comparing and synthesizing. And multiple-text reading just makes sense for most projects. Some of us have been using the term "text sets" to refer to these groups of topically related sources.

- **Don't get too worked up about text levels.** Recall from Chapter Two my point that an individual student probably does not consistently read at one particular level. Factors such as student interest and background knowledge can significantly affect a student's reading level. In fact, don't be surprised if you find students reading at a higher level when they've finished using a text set because of all the background knowledge they've gained and exposure to key words they've experienced. I'm not suggesting you should ignore the fit of the text for the reader, but rather that you should not be overly rigid about it.

- **Keep the level of scaffolding you can provide in mind.** Students can read more complex text with scaffolding. As you are choosing source texts, think about how much scaffolding you will be able to provide. If you have 20 students, a reading specialist, an ELL specialist, and four volunteers helping you (Wouldn't that be nice?!), you will probably be better able to support students with more difficult texts than if you have 35 students and no helpers. That said, there are many ways to provide scaffolding that do not require your physical presence. See pages 107–109 for some suggestions.

- **Imagine different kinds of source texts.** The most obvious kinds of source texts are those that provide information for use in the project—for example, a source text on scalloped hammerhead sharks for a project on endangered marine animals. However, don't rule out source texts that are more process-oriented, such as texts that teach how to conduct a survey or interview.

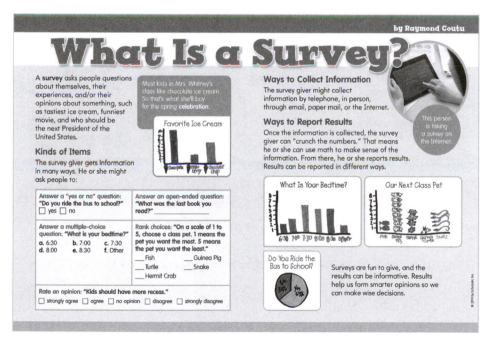

FIGURE 4.2: This source text explains how to conduct a survey (Coutu, 2014).

Sometimes source texts mainly provide context or inspiration for students. For example, colleagues and I have written a project in which first graders create their own flavored drinks and then write recipes (procedural texts) to share with others who would like to make the drink (in the process, students learn about observation, senses, solids, and liquids). Shown below is one of our source texts for that project. It is about food scientists and the role of taste testing in their work. Content from this text won't find its way into students' final product, but it will provide context and inspiration when they do some taste testing of their own as part of the project.

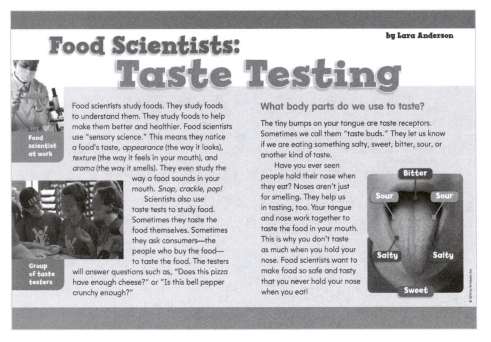

FIGURE 4.3: This source text explains what food scientists do (Anderson, 2014).

- **When all else fails, consider writing your own source texts.** Particularly if you teach in the primary grades, you may struggle to find appropriate source texts students can read themselves, even with a well-stocked book room and access to kid-friendly websites, such as those listed on page 92. One way to handle this is to write your own source texts at a level you think students will be able to read. This is easily done by taking an existing text and "writing it down" closer to your students' level, which may sound like a lot of work, but perhaps not as much work as the ongoing search for existing texts to use. Also, you can use these modified texts again if/when you repeat the project. Colleagues and I have applied this strategy for social studies units having to do with the local community, as there simply don't seem to be grade-appropriate texts available on that topic (Duke & Halvorsen, in progress).

I won't pretend that finding or developing source texts is easy, but if you're a literacy nerd (and if you're reading this book—guess what?—you are!), you will experience a great feeling of satisfaction when you find and/or develop just the right texts to support a project. Happy hunting!

TEXT SETS THROUGHOUT THE DAY

Text sets can be used during project time—and beyond. For example, if you use a guided-reading approach, rather than having students read a different, largely unrelated book each meeting, have them read sets of texts with a common thread (preferably related to any project they might be doing), such as the same topic or theme, author, or literary genre. If you use a core reading program, keep in mind that "themes" in most programs are often too broad to comprise true text sets. Consider reorganizing the order of selections or supplementing selections as needed to create text sets that extend and/or enhance any project-based work you might be doing.

How to Teach in the Reading and Research Phase

In this section, I focus on four fundamental practices that will help develop students' knowledge of and skills in reading and research:

1. The Gradual Release of Responsibility Model

2. Read-Aloud

3. Needs-Based Grouping

4. Smart Support

THE GRADUAL RELEASE OF RESPONSIBILITY MODEL

The gradual release of responsibility model refers to an approach to instruction in which students assume more responsibility for their application of knowledge or a strategy, as the teacher assumes less. Figure 4.4 shows a depiction of this model.

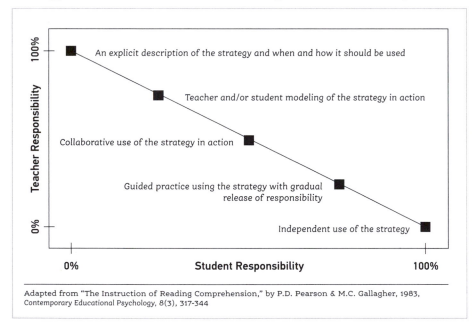

Adapted from "The Instruction of Reading Comprehension," by P.D. Pearson & M.C. Gallagher, 1983, Contemporary Educational Psychology, 8(3), 317-344

FIGURE 4.4: An adapted version of the gradual release of responsibility model
Note. From "Essential Elements of Fostering and Teaching Reading Comprehension" by Nell K. Duke, P. D. Pearson, S. L. Strachan, and A. K. Billman, 2011. In S. J. Samuels and A. E. Farstrup (Eds.), What Research Has to Say About Reading Instruction (4th ed.) (p. 65), Newark, DE: International Reading Association. Copyright 2011 by the International Reading Association. Reprinted with permission.

APPLYING THE GRADUAL RELEASE OF RESPONSIBILITY MODEL TO PROJECT-BASED SESSIONS: A 10-STEP APPROACH

Whole Class:

1. **Remind** students of the project purpose.

2. **Explain** to students how what they will be learning and doing in the session will contribute to achieving that purpose.

3. **Explicitly teach or review** specific knowledge and/or strategy/ies.

4. **Model** use of the knowledge or strategy/ies and/or engage students in modeling for one another.

Individually, in Pairs, or in Small Groups:

5. **Apply together the knowledge or strategy/ies** with students who need support.

6. **Coach** students as they work to apply the content or strategy/ies.

7. **Adjust the scaffolding and coaching** provided to each student based on the degree of independence that he or she can attain while still being successful. The goal should always be for students to move toward greater independence in reading and readiness for more difficult texts and tasks (which then will likely require a new cycle of scaffolding and coaching, and so on).

Wrap–Up:

8. **Review the knowledge or strategy/ies** presented at the beginning of the session.

9. **Point out strong examples** of students' application of the knowledge or strategy/ies.

10. **Note how students' hard work will serve their purpose or audience well.**

Of course, release does not occur only within a lesson. As the name of the model implies, this happens gradually, across lessons over time, as students take greater responsibility for applying the knowledge or strategy, and you spend less time explaining, modeling, or coaching. As texts and tasks become more complex, you cycle back to a greater level of responsibility.

The gradual release of responsibility model was first published by P. David Pearson and Margaret C. Gallagher in 1983. Since then, it has become a widely recommended approach to teaching comprehension strategies as well as many other instructional targets. As I write this, a Google search of the phrase "gradual release of responsibility" typed within quotation marks yields nearly a half-million hits. The What Works Clearinghouse panel included the recommendation to "Teach reading comprehension strategies by using a gradual release of responsibility" (Shanahan et al., 2010, p. 1). I do believe it is the single most effective approach to teaching not only comprehension strategies—in general and in particular—but also much of the knowledge and many of the strategies listed in the section "What to Teach in the Reading and Research Phase" on pages 76–97.

READ-ALOUD

Because most K–5 students' reading comprehension will not be as high as their listening comprehension until middle school or beyond, read-aloud plays an important role throughout elementary school. Reading aloud informational text provides students with exposure to content, syntax, and vocabulary that they simply can't grapple with entirely on their own. For that reason among others, it is an essential tool in the Reading and Research phase for building project-related knowledge and for developing informational reading and writing skills. In a typical project-based session as outlined in the box on page 99, read-aloud can often be used in steps 3 and 4:

- **Explicitly teach or review** specific knowledge and/or strategy/ies.

- **Model** use of the knowledge or strategy/ies and/or engage students in modeling for one another.

Whenever reading aloud to students it is important to:

- **Set a purpose** for the read-aloud that relates to the project. Help students understand why you are reading what you are reading, and how paying close attention contributes to the final product of the project.

- **Read with expression.** Don't reserve your best inflection and most engaging tone for stories alone. Good prosody helps students to process and engage with informational text as well. As a thought experiment, try reading the following sentence with different levels of inflection: "There are more than 400 species of sharks."

- **Ask questions** aligned with standards and other instructional goals. For example, to address CCSS Standard 6 for Reading Informational Text, second grade—"Identify the main purpose of a text, including what the author wants to answer, explain, or describe"—you might ask, "Why did the author write this text?" (For more questions to ask during reading, see pages 110–118.)

- **Give students opportunities to turn and talk.** During a turn and talk, each student turns to a classmate and has a brief conversation related to the question or topic at hand, as well as having opportunities for whole-class discussion.

- **Encourage critique.** The read-aloud is enhanced when students bring a critical lens to the experience. You can help them do that by asking questions such as,

"How does this text help us with our project?" "How does it fall short?" "How might the author have said that more effectively or differently?" When students see limitations of a text being read aloud or used in small group, encourage them to suggest ways to improve the text. They can use correction tape to add a caption that would clarify a photograph, insert sticky notes with better explanations of unfamiliar words, add an index or table of contents to support navigation, and so on.

How to Make a Paper Bag Puppet

Materials
- yarn
- glue
- plastic bag

Steps
1. Make a mouth by drawing lips above and below the flap.
2. Draw a nose and ears with markers.
3. To use the puppet, put your hand into the bag.
4. Lay the bag flat, with the flap facing up.
5. Glue two paper disks to the flap for eyes.

FIGURE 4.5: You can engage students in improving all text types—including procedural texts. This poorly written text, for example, offers several opportunities for improvement. Give it to your students and encourage them to make it shine!

- **Encourage note-taking.** Provide blank paper or graphic organizers on clipboards and have students take notes on information they can use in their project. Keep in mind, notes may be in the form of drawing for kindergartners and some first graders.

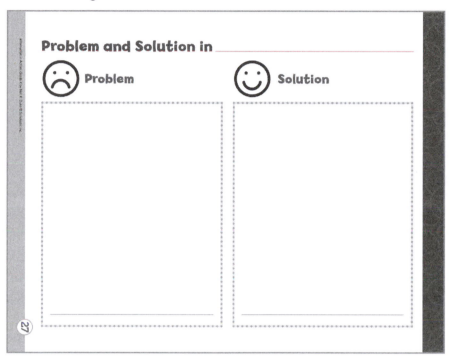

FIGURE 4.6: This note-taking sheet is designed to draw the attention of kindergarten students to the problem and solution in a text read aloud to them. Download a full-size version of this worksheet at http://umich.edu/~nkduke/.

- **Teach vocabulary.** I recommend the following approach to teaching vocabulary before, during, and after the read aloud—and beyond (drawing on Beck and McKeown, 2007, and Scanlon, Anderson, and Sweeney, 2010):

Before the read-aloud:

» Teach only words or concepts that are absolutely essential to understanding the text and aren't easily taught during the read-aloud. (There may be none, which is fine.)

During the read-aloud:

» Provide brief, child-friendly explanations of potentially unfamiliar words and concepts.

» Ask students to say the word with you, checking their pronunciation. Having students say the word aloud helps build a phonological representation of it in their memory, which helps with learning the word.

» If necessary, reread the text with a synonym and then go back to the original word.

» Encourage students to use the word during discussion of the text with you or turn and talk with a classmate.

After the read-aloud:

» If time does not permit reviewing all the words you explained during the read-aloud, prioritize those that are most expected and important for the grade level. For each word:

√ Reread from the point at which it occurs in the text.

√ Review its meaning.

√ Ask students to say it aloud again.

√ Give examples of other contexts or occasions in which it might be used.

√ Have students engage in a brief activity related to it. (For example, have them act out *prowling* or *prancing*, have them look for objects in the classroom that are aptly and not aptly described by the word, and so on.)

Later in the day, week, and year:

» Given that students need many exposures to a word in order to learn it, try to use unfamiliar words that appeared in the text on a natural, ongoing basis. (Some teachers keep a running list or use sticky notes to remind them to revisit specific words.)

» When you hear or see a student using the word, praise his or her use and point out that use to other students.

Keeping these suggestions in mind should help you make the most of read-aloud to build vocabulary.

TEACHING STUDENTS TO INFER WORD MEANING FROM CONTEXT

As indicated in the sections of this chapter focused on vocabulary (pages 90–91 and 103–105), we not only need to teach specific words to students, we also need to teach students to try to figure out what words mean from the context in which they're used. Below is an example of pages designed to do just that. They support small-group work in a second-grade project that involves an author study of Jim Arnosky. For the final product, students develop booklets on endangered marine animals and send them to preservation foundations that help endangered animals. The booklets are then distributed to the foundations' contributors.

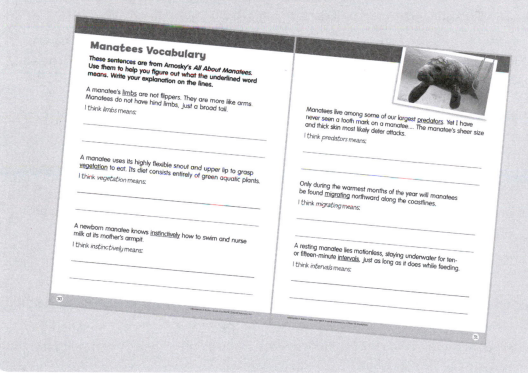

NEEDS-BASED GROUPING

In the U.S., ability grouping for reading, or level-based grouping as it's sometimes called, is extremely common. There are times when it is useful to group students based on their perceived reading level (recognizing that levels are only approximations and the level at which each student reads from one text to the next may vary considerably based on his or her interest, background knowledge, and other factors). However, this type of grouping assumes that students reading at the same level share the same instructional needs. This is not always—or perhaps even not often—the case, particularly when it comes to comprehension. Students can perform similarly on a reading comprehension assessment and yet have vastly different reading strengths and weaknesses (e.g., Riddle Buly & Valencia, 2002). For this and other reasons, I suggest needs-based grouping as the primary grouping strategy for project-based instruction. A student who is struggling to identify and make use of text structure might be grouped with classmates struggling with the same issue for instruction and support. The same is true for a student who is struggling with decoding multi-syllabic words, or a student who has chosen to study deep-sea creatures and is struggling with related vocabulary, and so on.

Admittedly, constructing needs-based groups can be overwhelming. Here are three approaches I have seen that ease the burden:

- The teacher has a stack of sticky notes and a writing utensil on hand when circulating during small group, partner, or individual time, and jots down particular needs of particular students on individual notes. Later, she sorts the sticky notes by needs to form groups for instruction.

- The teacher creates a grid with each student's name as the row headings and each target of instruction (e.g., specific CCSS, specific comprehension strategies) as the column headings, and attaches it to a clipboard. As she circulates during small group, partner, or individual time, she checks off students who have met specific targets of instruction and circles or highlights the cells of students who have not and, from there, groups them for additional instruction or support.

TABLE 8: SAMPLE GRID WITH TARGETS OF INSTRUCTION

Student	Targets of Instruction	
	CCSS: RI.5.1	Comprehension Strategy: Rereading
Jason	✓	✓
Sophie	⬭	⬭
Abril	✓	✓
Hannah	✓	✓
Diya	✓	✓
Caden	✓	⬭
Samantha	✓	✓
Dylan	⬭	⬭
Gerardo	✓	✓

- The teacher administers an assessment prior to a unit to form groups. For example, you might elicit a prompted writing sample (see pages 150–151) and then group students based on an element of writing they need to work on, such as writing a strong introduction or organizing information topically.

Whatever approach you use to form groups, needs-based grouping allows you to tailor your precious instructional time to each student's most pressing needs.

SMART SUPPORT

In my experience, one major factor that determines the success of a project is the degree to which the teacher provides each student with the support he or she needs to engage with and complete the project successfully. The following are K–2 support strategies designed for three populations: (1) students who need additional support, (2) students who need additional challenge, and (3) dual language learners. Some of these examples come directly from research, others are based on our classroom experiences. I want to particularly acknowledge Estanislado S. Barrera, IV, Raymond Coutu, Ellen Daugherty Durr, Sarah Glasscock, Jean Lawler, and Tammi Van Buren for their contributions to this list.

For Additional Support

- Assist students by creating an anchor chart with key words from the text and corresponding pictures to remind them of each word's pronunciation and meaning.

- Assist students by rereading the text to them or providing an audio recording of it.

- Engage students in rereading the text.

- Write easier-to-read versions of source texts. This can be done relatively quickly and will help students utilize a broader range of information.

- Have students work with a partner.

- Pull together a small group to provide extra support.

- Engage support teachers and volunteers in assisting students.

For Additional Challenge

- Have students extend their understanding of the audience by creating a profile of an audience member.

- Encourage students to do an Internet search to find out more about the topic featured in the launch or source texts. Or provide more challenging texts for them to examine.

- Ask students to share their ideas with a partner and discuss new ideas to share with the class.

- Think with students about an additional, related project they might carry out.

- Encourage students to compare and contrast words or illustrations in one text to a text on a similar subject written and/or illustrated in a different style (for example, in photographs). Have them list the pros and cons of both styles.

Reaching Dual Language Learners

- Bring in one or more examples of the project format (e.g., invitations, brochures, pamphlets) written in students' home language(s). (You can ask families for help with this.) Discuss the characteristics of the format.

- Provide opportunities for peers of the same language background to reread and discuss the source text together and then collaborate on note-taking.

- Give students the opportunity to watch a video or videos related to the text.

- Find a book about the topic that is written in the student's home language. Pair the student with another child who speaks the same language and let them compare the texts together, using the photos to help them visualize.

- Provide opportunities for peers of the same language background to work together in their home language.

These strategies will not, of course, apply to every project or every learner. I highly recommend that teachers of adjoining grade levels meet at the end of the year to share knowledge. Specifically, teacher(s) of the earlier grades should pass along to the teacher(s) of the later grade information about the support strategies that worked especially well for specific students. In keeping with the gradual release of responsibility model, the ultimate goal is for students to learn strategies they can use to help themselves with the challenges and opportunities that project-based instruction brings.

Instructional Techniques for CCSS: Don't Get Caught in a Rut!

There are so many instructional techniques that can be used to develop informational reading skills. In the table on pages 110–118, I take the CCSS Reading Standards 1–9 for Informational Text K–5 and suggest one example of an instructional technique you could use to help students meet the standards at each grade level. Please note that techniques listed at one grade level might be very useful at another grade level. My hope is that the variety of techniques will help to keep you from getting caught in a rut.

TABLE 9: INSTRUCTIONAL TECHNIQUES FOR K–5 READING INFORMATIONAL TEXT (CCSS)

Common Core State Standard	Possible Instructional Technique
Grade K	
RI.K.1 With prompting and support, ask and answer questions about key details in a text.	With nonfiction narrative text and some biographies, the 5 Ws plus H (*who, what, when, where, why, how*) can be a helpful heuristic. Place more emphasis on *why* and *how* questions than on the other questions.
RI.K.2 With prompting and support, identify the main topic and retell key details of a text.	Ask two key questions: 1. *What is this text mostly about?* 2. *What are the most important things the author has told us?* Have students use turn and talk to share their initial thinking, then discuss as a whole class.
RI.K.3 With prompting and support, describe the connection between two individuals, events, ideas, or pieces of information in a text.	Write several individuals, events, ideas, or pieces of information from a text on sentence strips. To help make the notion of connection concrete, use a chain, string, or building toy to literally connect the two.
RI.K.4 With prompting and support, ask and answer questions about unknown words in a text.	Place a penny or token in a jar each time a student asks about an unfamiliar word. After a certain number of tokens are earned, show an episode of "Word Girl," a vocabulary-building cartoon on PBS (http://pbskids.org/wordgirl/adventures).
RI.K.5 Identify the front cover, back cover, and title page of a book.	Arrange for a pre-K class, younger siblings, or other younger children to visit the class to get a well-practiced "lesson" from your students on front cover, back cover, and title page.
RI.K.6 Name the author and illustrator of a text and define the role of each in presenting the ideas or information in a text.	Write *author* and *illustrator* on arrow-shaped sticky notes. Give each student the opportunity to label the author and illustrator on a favorite classroom book. Have them turn and talk about the author's and illustrator's roles.

Common Core State Standard	Possible Instructional Technique
RI.K.7 With prompting and support, describe the relationship between illustrations and the text in which they appear (e.g., what person, place, thing, or idea in the text an illustration depicts).	Use large sticky notes to cover up the written words in a text. Have students speculate as to what the words might be based on the picture. Later in the text, do the same but cover up the pictures instead of the words.
RI.K.8 With prompting and support, identify the reasons an author gives to support points in a text.	Engage students in asking and discussing "Why?" after each key point the author makes. List answers for all to see.
RI.K.9 With prompting and support, identify basic similarities in and differences between two texts on the same topic (e.g., in illustrations, descriptions, or procedures).	Use hula hoops, word cards, and sentence strips to make an extra-large Venn diagram the class can complete during read-aloud of two texts on the same topic.
Grade 1	
RI.1.1 Ask and answer questions about key details in a text.	Give each student the opportunity to be "Questioner for a Day," asking peers one or more questions during read-aloud.
RI.1.2 Identify the main topic and retell key details of a text.	Engage students in taking notes (which may involve drawing pictures) about a text read aloud and use them to support a retelling about the text at home (or to an adult at school if the home context will not support this).
RI.1.3 Describe the connection between two individuals, events, ideas, or pieces of information in a text.	Provide clipboards with graphic organizers, such as a Venn diagram or chronological order chart, for students to complete and discuss as they listen to the text read aloud.
RI.1.4 Ask and answer questions to help determine or clarify the meaning of words and phrases in a text.	Give each student a sign, such as a wooden stick with a question mark, to hold up when they hear you read an unfamiliar word.

Common Core State Standard	Possible Instructional Technique
RI.1.5 Know and use various text features (e.g., headings, tables of contents, glossaries, electronic menus, icons) to locate key facts or information in a text.	Make a game of guessing what something is or means based on its icon. A good place to start is with an online drawing tool or app designed for children.
RI.1.6 Distinguish between information provided by pictures or other illustrations and information provided by the words in a text.	Consider introducing this concept with a story, such as Peggy Rathmann's *Officer Buckle and Gloria* (1995), in which the pictures convey very different information than the written words. Then transition to an informative/explanatory text in which the same is true, such as Steve Jenkins' *Actual Size* (2004).
RI.1.7 Use the illustrations and details in a text to describe its key ideas.	Divide the class into groups, with different groups reading or listening to texts on different topics. After groups have read and discussed their text, have them meet with another group to describe the text's details and key ideas from illustrations and written words.
RI.1.8 Identify the reasons an author gives to support points in a text.	Engage students in completing a graphic organizer in which they identify the key points and reasons to support them. Students can use the organizer to help plan their own writing.
RI.1.9 Identify basic similarities in and differences between two texts on the same topic (e.g., in illustrations, descriptions, or procedures).	Explain to students that you could not decide which book to use to introduce a particular concept or task. Read both and engage students in discussing how they are similar and different, which is better suited to the concept or task, and why.
Grade 2	
RI.2.1 Ask and answer such questions as who, what, where, when, why, and how to demonstrate understanding of key details in a text.	Provide a graphic organizer with the 5 Ws plus H. This tends to work best with nonfiction narrative text and some biographies.

Common Core State Standard	Possible Instructional Technique
RI.2.2 Identify the main topic of a multi-paragraph text as well as the focus of specific paragraphs within the text.	Engage students in making headings to insert into a text (with paragraphs) that is topically organized but lacks headings.
RI.2.3 Describe the connection between a series of historical events, scientific ideas or concepts, or steps in technical procedures in a text.	Engage students in using a flow chart to represent the cause-and-effect relationships among a series of historical events. There are many online flow-chart-making tools and templates.
RI.2.4 Determine the meaning of words and phrases in a text relevant to a *grade 2 topic or subject area.*	Teach definitions as one fundamental type of context clue. Baumann, Edwards, Boland, Olejnik, and Kame'enui (2003) provide this example: "When the sun hit its **zenith**, which means *right overhead*, I could tell it was noon by the tremendous heat" (p. 464). (See this cell/standard for each of grades 3–5.)
RI.2.5 Know and use various text features (e.g., captions, bold print, subheadings, glossaries, indexes, electronic menus, icons) to locate key facts or information in a text efficiently.	Identify texts in the classroom that lack glossaries or indexes and engage students in creating them to clip to the text for future students' use.
RI.2.6 Identify the main purpose of a text, including what the author wants to answer, explain, or describe.	Include the question "Why did the author write this text?" within each read-aloud. When available, use an online video of the author answering that question.
RI.2.7 Explain how specific images (e.g., a diagram showing how a machine works) contribute to and clarify a text.	Use sticky notes to cover an image in the text being read aloud. Read the written text and ask children what they can learn from it alone. Then uncover the image and ask students what more they can learn.
RI.2.8 Describe how reasons support specific points the author makes in a text.	Use a graphic organizer similar to grade 1, but engage students in exploring the lines connecting key points to reasons and in making notes about the connections.
RI.2.9 Compare and contrast the most important points presented by two texts on the same topic.	Engage students in constructing a T-chart comparing the two texts. Under each title, list the top three points the author makes in the text. Compare lists to see which points do and do not overlap.

Common Core State Standard	Possible Instructional Technique
Grade 3	
RI.3.1 Ask and answer questions to demonstrate understanding of a text, referring explicitly to the text as the basis for the answers.	Establish a consistent follow-up question, such as, "How do you know?" that students are asked after they initially respond to a question. Encourage students to ask this question of you and one another. Eventually, they are likely to automatically include how they know in their initial responses.
RI.3.2 Determine the main idea of a text; recount the key details and explain how they support the main idea.	Pair students based on a common interest. Invite them to find two texts on that topic. Have each student read one of the texts and plan a retelling aligned with the standard to share with his or her partner.
RI.3.3 Describe the relationship between a series of historical events, scientific ideas or concepts, or steps in technical procedures in a text, using language that pertains to time, sequence, and cause/effect.	Create anchor charts with key words pertaining to time, sequence, and cause and effect. Model use of, and remind students to use, these words in their discussion of a text.
RI.3.4 Determine the meaning of general academic and domain-specific words and phrases in a text relevant to a *grade 3 topic or subject area*.	Teach the synonym—another type of context clue identified by Baumann et al. (2003), as in: "Captain Jackson's uniform was **impeccable**. In fact, it was so *perfect* that she always had the highest score during inspection" (p. 464).
RI.3.5 Use text features and search tools (e.g., key words, sidebars, hyperlinks) to locate information relevant to a given topic efficiently.	Engage students in brainstorming key words related to the project topic. Have students guess which key word will get them the most relevant site as the top hit. Then go through the searches with students to identify the "winner."
RI.3.6 Distinguish their own point of view from that of the author of a text.	Engage students in completing a T-chart with one column for "I think" and a second for "The author thinks."
RI.3.7 Use information gained from illustrations (e.g., maps, photographs) and the words in a text to demonstrate understanding of the text (e.g., where, when, why, and how key events occur).	Create a three-column chart listing the 5Ws plus H in the first column. Add columns for students to briefly explain what they learned and to indicate where in the text they found that information. Engage students in comparing organizers to see whether they are finding the information in different places.

Common Core State Standard	Possible Instructional Technique
RI.3.8 Describe the logical connection between particular sentences and paragraphs in a text (e.g., comparison, cause/effect, first/second/third in a sequence).	Provide photocopies or digital copies of a text that students can mark up. Allow them to use circling, lines, and highlighting to show the connections among different parts of the text. I suggest beginning with conceptually simple texts with just one kind of logical connection.
RI.3.9 Compare and contrast the most important points and key details presented in two texts on the same topic.	Repeat the activity for this standard in grade 2, but add key details.
Grade 4	
RI.4.1 Refer to details and examples in a text when explaining what the text says explicitly and when drawing inferences from the text.	Teach students to use the heuristic "The text says . . . I know . . . And so . . ." to explain their inferences.
RI.4.2 Determine the main idea of a text and explain how it is supported by key details; summarize the text.	Introduce book reviews as an authentic reason for students to construct strong summaries of texts. Have students begin their reviews with a summary and then provide a response or critique.
RI.4.3 Explain events, procedures, ideas, or concepts in a historical, scientific, or technical text, including what happened and why, based on specific information in the text.	Invite students to select and read a text they believe will be of interest to a member of their family (or that is relevant to a specific project). Then ask them to plan an explanation of events, procedures, ideas, or concepts to share with the family member.
RI.4.4 Determine the meaning of general academic and domain-specific words or phrases in a text relevant to a *grade 4 topic or subject area*.	Teach the antonym—another type of context clue identified by Baumann et al. (2003), as in: "The soldier was very **intrepid** in battle, in contrast to the person next to him who was quite *cowardly*" (p. 464).

Common Core State Standard	Possible Instructional Technique
RI.4.5 Describe the overall structure (e.g., chronology, comparison, cause/effect, problem/solution) of events, ideas, concepts, or information in a text or part of a text.	Ask a teacher of a younger grade level to come in and tell students she/he needs good examples of texts with these four text structures (which is probably true!). Give students time to read a series of texts on- or offline, identify their structures, and select one for each text structure as good examples for the teacher.
RI.4.6 Compare and contrast a firsthand and secondhand account of the same event or topic; describe the differences in focus and the information provided.	Provide a T-chart with column headings by firsthand and secondhand account. Engage students in completing the chart as they read multiple accounts of the same event or topic.
RI.4.7 Interpret information presented visually, orally, or quantitatively (e.g., in charts, graphs, diagrams, time lines, animations, or interactive elements on Web pages) and explain how the information contributes to an understanding of the text in which it appears.	Give students the opportunity to read online magazine articles (see list of possible sites on page 92) likely to incorporate one or more of these elements. Ask students to present to the class or a group about a particular element they found and how it contributes to meaning in the text in which it appears.
RI.4.8 Explain how an author uses reasons and evidence to support particular points in a text.	Have students use highlighters (or a digital highlighting tool) to identify reasons and evidence within a text. Have partners compare their highlighting.
RI.4.9 Integrate information from two texts on the same topic in order to write or speak about the subject knowledgeably.	Provide two texts, perhaps of different formats, such as an interview transcript and an article, for students to integrate for the purposes of a project.

Common Core State Standard	Possible Instructional Technique
Grade 5	
RI.5.1 Quote accurately from a text when explaining what the text says explicitly and when drawing inferences from the text.	Teach students the phrase "and I quote" and encourage and praise its use during class discussion. If possible, show one or more videos in which adults use that same device.
RI.5.2 Determine two or more main ideas of a text and explain how they are supported by key details; summarize the text.	Revisit book reviewing from Grade 4, focusing on texts of greater complexity in terms of density of ideas.
RI.5.3 Explain the relationships or interactions between two or more individuals, events, ideas, or concepts in a historical, scientific, or technical text based on specific information in the text.	In small-group and large-group discussions, have students repeatedly pose and address the question "What does what we just read have to do with what we read earlier?"
RI.5.4 Determine the meaning of general academic and domain-specific words and phrases in a text relevant to a *grade 5 topic or subject area.*	Teach the example—another type of context clue identified by Baumann et al. (2003), as in: "*Tigers, lions, panthers, and leopards* are some of the most beautiful members of the **feline** family" (p. 464).
RI.5.5 Compare and contrast the overall structure (e.g., chronology, comparison, cause/effect, problem/solution) of events, ideas, concepts, or information in two or more texts.	Identify a project during the course of the year in which students are likely to use different structures in their writing. Engage students in comparing and contrasting the structure of their writing with that of a classmate.
RI.5.6 Analyze multiple accounts of the same event or topic, noting important similarities and differences in the point of view they represent.	Support students in developing and completing a multi-column chart with a column for each account.
RI.5.7 Draw on information from multiple print or digital sources, demonstrating the ability to locate an answer to a question quickly or to solve a problem efficiently.	Have students submit things they wonder about to a "Wonder Jar." Model addressing that wonder through a digital search that checks two or more relevant sources. Then assign small groups or pairs of students to address other wonderings in the jar.

Common Core State Standard	Possible Instructional Technique
RI.5.8 Explain how an author uses reasons and evidence to support particular points in a text, identifying which reasons and evidence support which point(s).	Engage students in highlighting a point, reasons, and evidence in the text that are connected. Then provide a different colored highlighter for a different point, reasons, and evidence, and so on.
RI.5.9 Integrate information from several texts on the same topic in order to write or speak about the subject knowledgeably.	Design a project in which students are reading three or more texts on the same topic and presenting the integration of information of these texts orally and/or in writing. Many projects referenced in this book would provide that opportunity.

Concluding Thoughts: Have Faith in Your Students and Yourself

By this point in the book, you may be more than a little overwhelmed—so many targets of instruction, so much to expect our students not only to learn, but also to apply in real-world situations. Here's some mid-book encouragement: Tammi Van Buren, who observed and worked with teachers implementing project-based units that colleagues and I designed, wrote to say that common responses teachers had when reading over lesson plans before teaching them was, "This is going to be too hard for the kids" and "They are not going to understand this." Tammi wrote, "I just smile and ask them to give it a try, letting them know they might be pleasantly surprised. At the end of the unit, the teachers are always surprised at what their students can do and how hard they have worked during the entire unit." So I ask you to remember the faith in children that brought you to this profession in the first place, and seize the opportunity to support them as they rise to the occasion.

CHAPTER FIVE The Writing and Research Phase

The project has been launched, students have conducted extensive research on the topic, and now it's time for them to further plan and begin drafting their project. In this chapter, I focus on instructional targets for writing and then present some general principles for teaching students to plan and draft text.

What to Teach in the Writing and Research Phase

Three targets of instruction for the Writing and Research Phase are especially important:

1. Standards

2. Writing Strategies and Text Structure

3. Other Text Features, Including Graphics

STANDARDS

There are so many aspects of writing—genre, format, style, mechanics, handwriting, et cetera—so it is important to consider what your state expects when it comes to writing—the state's standards. The CCSS contains three central pages on writing for the elementary grades: pages 19, 20, and 21. Standard 1 is always about persuasive writing (using the term "opinion" early on, then "argument" later), Standard 2 is always about informative/explanatory writing, and Standard 3 is always about narrative (fiction or nonfiction narrative) writing. The remainder of the standards has to do with how the writing is produced—the development and organization of the writing (Standard 4); the planning, revising, and editing of the writing (also mentioned is completely rewriting or trying a new approach) (Standard 5); the use of technology and collaboration for writing (Standard 6); the research and analysis that goes into writing (Standards 7 through 9); and the time frame and range of the writing (Standard 10).

PENCIL TO PAPER/FINGERS TO KEYS

In Chapter Four I discussed the importance of ensuring that students have lots of time for eyes on print. The analogy in writing is time for pencil to paper or fingers to keys. More effective teachers tend to have their students writing more of the time (e.g., Pressley et al., 2001). In a project-based approach, students may be writing not only the final product, but also various texts that prepare them for writing the final product, such as summaries of source texts and letters to potential interviewees. Of course, students may be writing during other parts of the day, entirely outside the realm of the project. Regardless of when they're writing, it's important to establish a purpose and an audience for their writing. Perhaps you have arranged for ongoing pen pal relationships for students through a site such as ePals, http://www.epals.com. Perhaps you engage students in generating a weekly or monthly newsletter for families and other members of the school community (see page 181). Perhaps you have students keep a dialogue journal (a journal in which you and each student communicate privately about his or her learning, classroom life, books he or she has read, emerging interests, and so on). All of these can increase students' time with pencil to paper or fingers to keys.

The Presentation of Knowledge and Ideas strand of the Speaking and Listening CCSS does not specifically refer to writing, but it does involve the production of oral and/or visual text and may involve production of written text (e.g., PowerPoint slides with written and visual text used in a presentation; note cards used to aid in a presentation). Indeed, when students present their final products of a project during the Presentation and Celebration phase, they may well be addressing Speaking and Listening standards, as well as Writing standards.

Finally, the Language standards also have relevance to the Writing and Research phase. Language Standard 1 at elementary always begins with: "Demonstrate command of the conventions of standard English grammar and usage when writing or speaking," with the conventions expected varying from grade level to grade level. Language Standard 2 at elementary always begins with: "Demonstrate command of the conventions of standard English capitalization, punctuation, and spelling when writing," again with the specific conventions that follow varying from grade level to grade level. Standard 3, which begins in grade 3, always starts with: "Use knowledge of language and its conventions when writing, speaking, reading, or listening." Standard 6 is also relevant to the Writing and Research and Revision and Editing phases. It deals with acquisition and use of specific words or phases, with vocabulary dependent on the grade level.

I can't stress enough the importance of digging deeply into the details of standards in identifying targets of instruction/lessons; guiding and responding to students' writing in small groups, pairs, or one-on-one; and ultimately in assessing their writing. I have seen too many projects for which there is a compelling purpose and audience, lots of excitement, and engagement, even use of mentor texts, but in the end, when I look at the writing relative to the CCSS, it falls short.

> **WHEN SHOULD STUDENTS LEARN TO TYPE?**
>
> The CCSS expect students to begin using digital tools for writing beginning in kindergarten, so when to teach students to type becomes a key question. The What Works Clearinghouse *Practice Guide on Teaching Elementary School Students to Be Effective Writers* (Graham et al., 2012) indicates that "Students should learn how to type fluently, preferably without looking at the keyboard" and specifically that "Students should be introduced to typing in first grade. By second grade, students should begin regular typing practice. By the end of second or third grade, students should be able to type as fast as they can write by hand" (p. 32). Fortunately, there are many programs for teaching touch typing to children, some of which are web-based so students can access them from any Internet-enabled keyboarded device, rather than just during school hours.

WRITING STRATEGIES AND TEXT STRUCTURE

It is just not enough to give students time to go through each phase of a writing process. We have to teach them how to go through those phases: We have to teach writing strategies. Recall from Chapter Two that a meta-analysis found that a writing-process approach to instruction has no impact on struggling writers (Graham & Sandmel, 2011). Struggling writers may need more instructional support than a writing-process approach provides. Among other things, struggling writers—as do writers in general—benefit from instruction in writing strategies. In fact, in another meta-analysis, looking at 115 studies of writing interventions for elementary-age students, strategy instruction had the greatest positive effect (Graham, McKeown, Kiuhara, & Harris, 2012).

The table below shows examples of generic strategies that can apply to different kinds of writing. Other strategies are specific to individual genres.

TABLE 10: EXAMPLES OF GENERIC WRITING STRATEGIES

Component of the Writing Process	Writing Strategy	How Students Can Use the Strategy	Grade Range
Planning	POW	▪ **P**ick ideas (i.e., decide what to write about). ▪ **O**rganize their notes (i.e., brainstorm and organize possible writing ideas into a writing plan). ▪ **W**rite and say more (i.e., continue to modify the plan while writing).	1–6
	Ordering ideas/outlining	▪ Brainstorm/generate ideas for their paper. ▪ Review their ideas and place a number by what will go first, second, third, and so on.	1–2
		▪ Brainstorm/generate ideas for their paper. ▪ Decide which are main ideas and which are supporting ideas. ▪ Create an outline that shows the order of the main ideas and the supporting details for each main idea.	3–6
Drafting	Imitation	▪ Select a sentence, paragraph, or text excerpt and imitate the author's form (see Recommendation 2b, examples 2 and 3).	1–6
	Sentence generation	▪ Try out sentences orally before writing them on paper. ▪ Try multiple sentences and choose the best one. ▪ Use transition words to develop different sentence structures. ▪ Practice writing good topic sentences.	3–6
Sharing	Peer sharing[35]	▪ In pairs, listen and read along as the author reads aloud. ▪ Share feedback with their writing partner, starting with what they liked.	2–6
	"Author's Chair"	▪ Sit in a special chair in front of peers and read their writing (see Recommendation 4, example 6, for more detail).	K–6

Evaluating	Self-evaluating	▪ Reread and ask these questions:
		  • Are the ideas clear?
		  • Is there a clear beginning, middle, and end?
		  • Does the writing connect with the reader?
		  • Are sentence types varied?
			2–6

	Self-monitoring	▪ Self-assess and ask these questions, either out loud or internally:
		  • Did I meet the goals I developed for my writing? If not, what changes should I make to meet my goals?
		  • Did I correctly use strategies that were appropriate for this task? If not, what should I change?
		▪ Record their answers to self-assessment questions on a chart or teacher-provided questionnaire in order to track their progress toward writing goals and strategy use.
		▪ Congratulate themselves, and inform their teacher, when they meet their goals.
			3–6

Revising and editing	Peer revising[36]	▪ Place a question mark (?) by anything they do not understand in their writing partner's paper. ▪ Place a carat (^) anywhere it would be useful to have the author include more information.	2–6

	COPS (editing)	▪ Ask the COPS editing questions:
		  • Did I **C**apitalize the first word in sentences and proper names?
		  • How is the **O**verall appearance of my paper?
		  • Did I use commas and end-of-sentence **P**unctuation?
		  • Did I **S**pell each word correctly?
			2–6

Note. From *Teaching Elementary School Students to Be Effective Writers: A Practice Guide* (p. 16) by S. Graham, A. Bollinger, C. Booth Olson, C. D'Aoust, C. MacArthur, D. McCutheon, and N. Olinghouse, 2012, Washington, D.C: National Center for Education and Evaluation and Regional Assistance, Institute of Education Sciences, U.S. Department of Education

Some writing strategies are also genre specific. As you will see below, many genre-specific strategies deal with text structure, which is why this section addresses both topics. In the meta-analysis mentioned earlier in this section, text structure instruction showed a strong effect. The following are some examples of a genre-specific strategy for each of the genres addressed in this book:

Informative/explanatory: Remember learning to outline when you were in school—Roman numeral I, capital letter A, and so on? We can offer elementary-age children a broader range of strategies. Mapping, as illustrated on page 127 for biography, is a good strategy for organizing information and planning informative/explanatory writing. Once the map is completed, students can use numbering to indicate which topics will be discussed and when. If you want students to incorporate graphics into their plans, a page layout outline might be helpful.

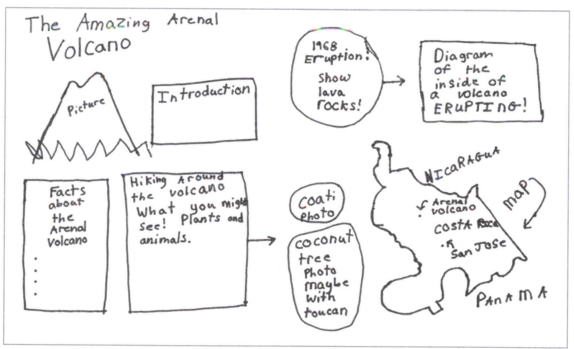

FIGURE 5.1: A student's page layout outline on the Arenal volcano in Costa Rica

Closely related to this strategy is using a template for organizing information and planning an informative/explanatory text. The example below shows a template for a booklet on an endangered species.

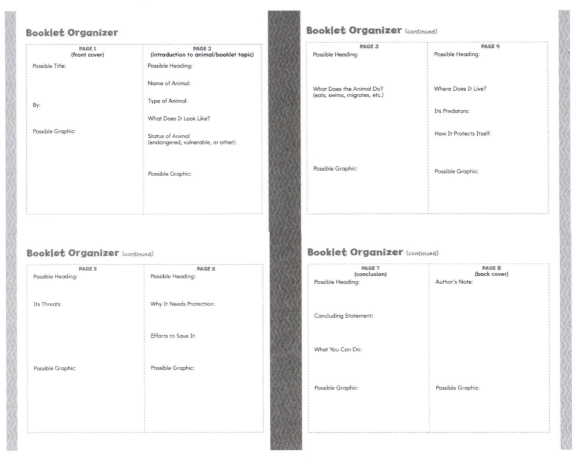

FIGURE 5.2: A template for a student booklet on an endangered species

When students are younger, it may make sense to simply provide the template for them. As they get older, they can work with you to create the template, using their understanding of a mentor text(s) and their preliminary ideas about what they want to include.

Persuasive: Researching the audience is an essential strategy in the initial stage of developing persuasive text; what might be compelling reasons and evidence for one audience may not be as much so for another. A long-standing genre-specific strategy for composing persuasive text, shown to be effective in grades 2 through 6, is TREE (Graham & Harris, 1989):

Tell what you believe. (State a topic sentence.)

Provide three or more **R**easons.

End it. (Wrap it up right.)

Examine. (Do I have all my parts?) (For older students, move this E before End it and change it to **E**xplain reasons. [Say more about each reason.])

Or you may find you want to use a structure more tightly aligned with the terminology and expectations of the CCSS (which, depending on the grade level, might include the following):

- Introduction
- Opinion
- Reasons
- Support for reasons
- Linking words
- Concluding statement or section

(Teach a mnemonic, such as **I**vy **O**nly **R**eads **S**uper **L**ong **C**omics, to help students remember the structure!)

Another option is to teach a problem-solution structure for persuasive writing, as in:

- Introduction
- Problem
    - » Description of the problem
    - » Evidence of the problem

- Solution

  » Reasons why this is a good solution

  » Support for reasons

- Concluding statement or section

Nonfiction narrative: Using a timeline with nonfiction narrative may be a useful strategy for planning and organizing the text. Studies also suggest that using a story-mapping tool, with questions similar to these, is helpful:

- **W**ho are the people involved? (I think it is best not to use the term "characters" with nonfiction.)

- **W**hen does the story take place?

- **W**here does the story take place?

- **W**hat is the problem?

- **W**hat do the people do about it?

- **H**ow does the problem get resolved?

As with revising and editing strategies, which are discussed in Chapter Six, we eventually want students to internalize writing strategies. That is, we don't want students to have to rely on a teacher to remind them to include an introduction, an opinion, reasons, and a conclusion in a piece of persuasive writing; we want them to be able to produce those on their own. In some cases, students may internalize the structure through experience in reading and writing it; other times a mnemonic such as TREE on the previous page may be helpful.

DOUBLE-DUTY GRAPHIC ORGANIZERS

Lessons on structure allow us to do double duty, addressing both reading and writing expectations. You can take advantage of this by using the same or similar graphic organizers to support reading and writing of the same genre. In the case of reading, students complete the graphic organizer based on the text they are reading. With writing, students complete the graphic organizer with the content they will include in their writing.

Biography: Here are two good writing strategies to consider with biography:

1. Using a map to organize information and plan the writing

2. Using a timeline to organize information and plan the writing

A map makes sense if the biography is going to be organized by topic, whereas a timeline can be preferable for a chronologically organized biography.

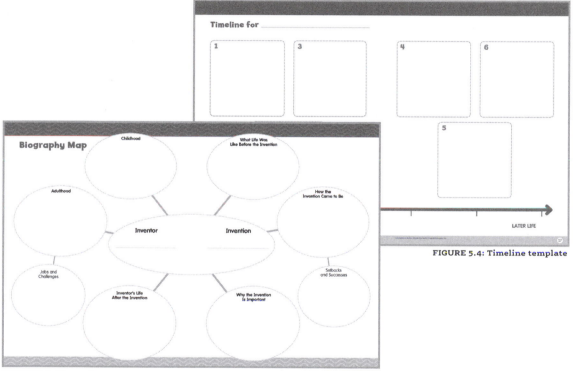

FIGURE 5.4: Timeline template

FIGURE 5.3: Biography map

Procedural: Procedural text is a great illustration of why I don't like saying "the writing process"—the writing process for procedural text is likely to differ from some other forms of text. Writing procedural text often involves actually doing the procedure, sometimes several times, while taking notes or videotaping.

Teaching the following procedural-text structure to elementary-age children is a supportive strategy:

- Title (which usually indicates the purpose of the procedure)
- Sometimes: A persuasive introduction—Why do this procedure?
- Materials
- Steps/procedures
- Sometimes: Tip(s)
- Sometimes: Warning(s)

A template such as this one can support students in using and learning this structure.

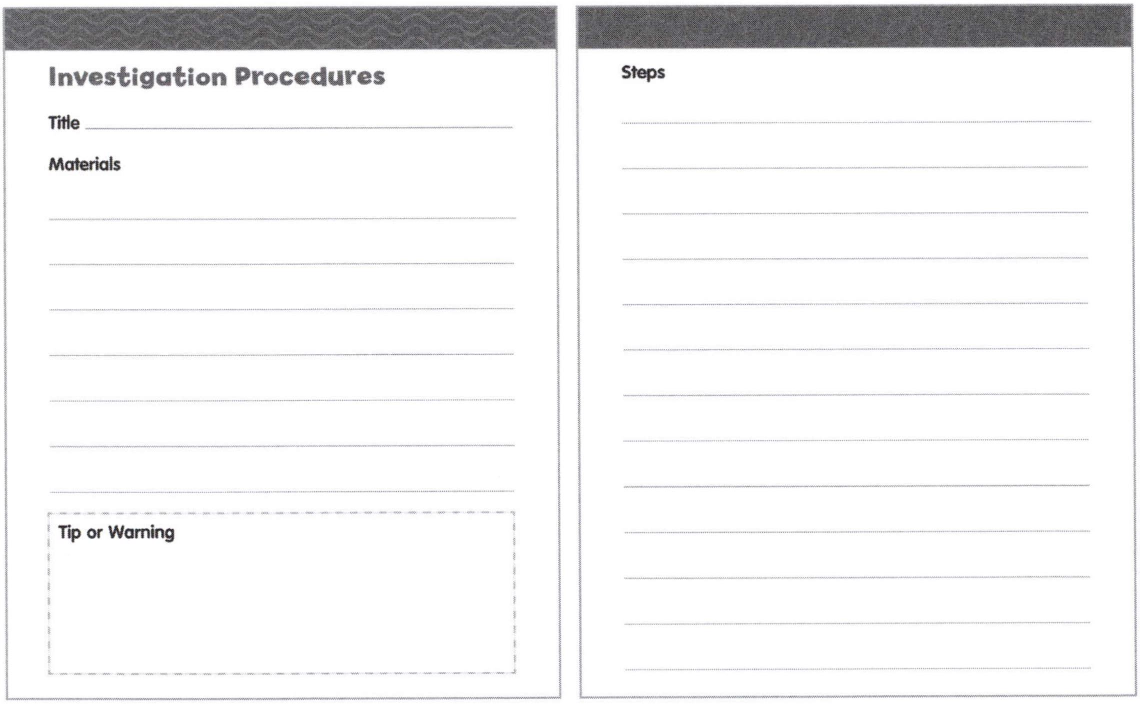

Investigation Procedures

Title _____

Materials

_____

_____

_____

_____

_____

Tip or Warning

Steps

_____

_____

_____

_____

_____

_____

_____

_____

_____

_____

_____

_____

_____

FIGURE 5.5: Procedural text template

Students study graphs in a source text.

OTHER TEXT FEATURES, INCLUDING GRAPHICS

Just as students can use knowledge of text features to support their reading (see pages 84–89), so too can they use text features to support their writing. Duke, Caughlan, Juzwik, and Martin (2012) drew from a variety of studies and sources to identify features of persuasive, procedural, informative/explanatory, narrative, and dramatic genres. We identified many dozens of features! Teaching all of these features is neither practical nor advisable. Rather, for any given project, I recommended focusing on just a couple of text features that (a) are expected in the standards or seem reasonable for the age and/or (b) you notice many students are not yet using, and (c) are well illustrated in the mentor text(s) you are using. For example, in first grade the CCSS expect students to be able to use glossaries in their reading, thus it might make sense to engage students in creating a glossary if they are writing a type of text that would authentically have one. Not all features worth teaching are specifically named in standards. For example, the CCSS do not specifically reference using graphics as a tool to persuade, but this is something I begin to teach in kindergarten or first grade. Similarly, you may notice that some of your students are trying to write procedural text like a story (*I put some sugar in the water. Then I put in some salt . . .*). Thus you might teach the use of imperative verbs (or "bossy words") in procedural texts (e.g., *Put the sugar in the water. Add some salt.*). Table 11 on the next page lists some of the key features you might find the need to teach, but please understand that they are just *some* of the key features. Your state's standards, mentor texts, and your observations of students' writing may point you to a number of additional standards to teach.

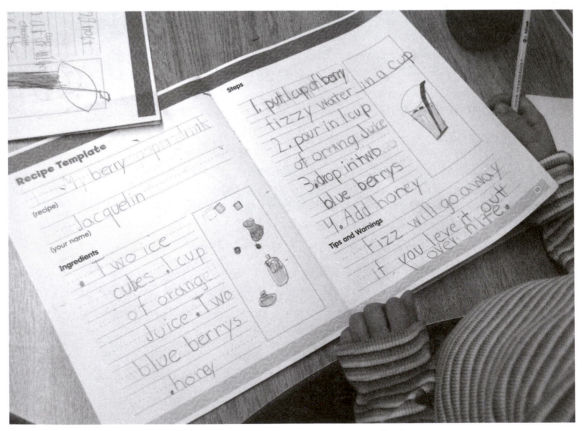

A student uses "bossy words" in her draft of a procedural text.

TABLE 11: NON-STRUCTURAL FEATURES YOU MIGHT TEACH
(See "Writing Strategies and Text Structure" on pages 121–128 for structural features.)

	Some Common Language Characteristics*	Some Common Graphical Characteristics*	Some Common Navigational Characteristics*

Informative/ Explanatory	• precise language (e.g., *sleep for 22 hours a day on average* vs. *are big sleepers*)
	
	• language referring to whole groups (e.g., *Dogs*, not *Rover* or *The little dog*)
	
	• language referring to timeless processes (e.g., *build underground burrows* vs. *built an underground burrow* or *was building an underground burrow*)
	
	• terms commonly associated with specific academic disciplines (e.g., *era, orbit, photosynthesis*)
	
	• definitions or explanations of words or phrases in running text and/or glossary (e.g., *Drought, or a long period with unusually little rain or other precipitation . . .*)
	
	• frequent use of a word or phrase that is the topic of a text (e.g., *volcanoes* in a book about volcanoes)
		• photographs or realistic (rather than fantastical) illustrations
		
		• labels and/or captions for graphics
		
		• highlighting, boldfacing, and italicizing words or phrases
		
		• graphical devices as on page 83
			• features for navigating printed text:
			  » table of contents
			  » headings and subheadings
			  » page numbers
			  » index
			
			• features for navigating digital text:
			  » search box
			  » scroll bars
			  » electronic outlines or menus
			  » hyperlinks
			  » bookmarks
			  » icons

	Some Common Language Characteristics*	**Some Common Graphical Characteristics***	**Some Common Navigational Characteristics***
Persuasive	(Please note: A more academic argument, as in a paper for history class, for example, is less likely to have some of these language features.) • linking words (e.g., *second, another, because, also, in fact, for example*) • words signaling disagreement (e.g., *but, however, actually*) • words qualifying a claim (e.g., *most, often, sometimes*) • imperative verbs (e.g., *Don't let them fool you!*) • questions, often rhetorical (e.g., *Do you want to do something good for the earth?*) • use of a range of pronouns: » you (e.g., *You don't want your community to . . .*) » we, us, our (e.g., *People who love their community like we do . . .*; invokes commonality with the audience) » they, them (e.g., *They just don't understand . . .*; invokes a sense of distance from or an "othering" of the opposing point of view)	• graphics that are intended to provide evidence or other support of a claim: » of a problem (e.g., a picture of a polluted lake; a map showing areas affected by a problem) » of the promise of a solution (e.g., a lake after a clean-up effort; a graph showing improvement after an intervention) • graphics that are intended to invoke an emotional response in the direction of the argument (e.g., an animal covered in oil; people marching arm-in-arm)	These may vary from no navigational features at all to any of the features listed in this column for Informative/Explanatory.

	Some Common Language Characteristics*	Some Common Graphical Characteristics*	Some Common Navigational Characteristics*
Biography and Nonfiction Narrative	• temporal terms (e.g., *in 1961; eventually; all of a sudden*) • third-person pronouns (e.g., *he, she, they, it*) • descriptive language » about a person (e.g., *a tall man, with a brilliant mind*) » about a setting (e.g., *dry and desolate*) » about events (e.g., *shook the walls and floors; poured onto the streets*) • direct quotations	• photos and/or illustrations of the subject • facsimiles of artifacts from the person's life or the events recounted	These may vary from no navigational features at all to any of the features listed in this column for *Informative/Explanatory*.

	Some Common Language Characteristics*	Some Common Graphical Characteristics*	Some Common Navigational Characteristics*

Procedural	• precise language and details, for example:
	  » units of measure indicating how much of a material is needed (e.g., *3 ml of water*)
	  » adjectives used to describe characteristics of material (e.g., *moist, gray clay*)
	  » prepositional phrases (e.g., *after 30 minutes; inside the cylinder*)
	• imperative verbs (e.g., *Drop . . .; Attach . . .*)
	• no personal pronoun or use of *you* only
	• indicators of the order of steps in the procedure (e.g., numbers, letters, or, less often, temporal terms such as *first . . ., next . . .*)
		• graphic of the end product (e.g., the completed dish, the expected result of the science investigation)
		• graphics showing each step or some key steps
			• headings
			  » what you need (e.g., *Materials, Ingredients*)
			  » what you do (e.g., *Steps, Procedures*)
			  » tips
			  » warnings
			  » explanations
			• subheadings for clusters of steps
			• materials listed, often, in order of use

* A given text may not necessarily, and need not, have all these features.

Note. This table draws on Duke, Caughlan, Juzwik, and Martin (2012); Purcell-Gates, Duke, and Martineau (2007); and my own observations.

It is so important not to teach features in isolation, but rather to teach them in the context of texts that students are reading and writing, emphasizing the purpose of each feature. It's relatively natural to do this in a project-based context, as you can make reference to the project purpose and audience and how a specific feature achieves that purpose and addresses that audience.

How to Teach in the Writing and Research Phase

Once again I am faced with a topic on which one could easily write (and many have written!) an entire book, but here are a few fundamental practices that will help develop students' writing and research knowledge and skills:

1. The Gradual Release of Responsibility Model

2. Modeled Writing, Mentor Texts, and Author Studies

3. Interactive Writing and Scaffolded Writing

4. Assessment and Needs-Based Grouping

5. Smart Support

You may notice that this list is similar to the one in the Reading and Research chapter. That is entirely intentional. Not only does research point to similar practices as effective to support reading and writing development, but also using similar practices seems likely to further foster synergy between reading and writing.

THE GRADUAL RELEASE OF RESPONSIBILITY MODEL

The gradual release of responsibility model, explained in Chapter Four on pages 98–100, has been recommended for use in writing as well, again in part because it has been used in so many interventions that have proven to be effective (Graham et al., 2012). The table on page 136 provides one depiction of its application to writing.

TABLE 12: GRADUAL RELEASE OF RESPONSIBILITY TO STUDENTS

Sharing Responsibility for the Task

Gradual Release of the Brainstorming Strategy

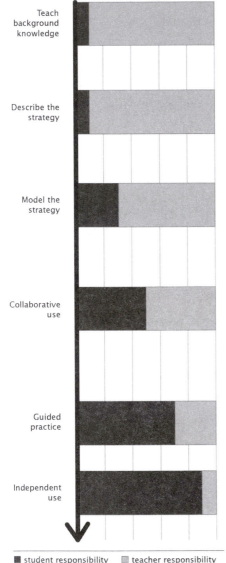

The teacher provides background knowledge, including why students should use the strategy and how it will help them: "What you write will be more interesting for others to read if you have a lot of good ideas, so you should take the time to write down all your ideas before you get started. One way to do this is to use a strategy called *brainstorming*. In brainstorming, you write down as many ideas as you can think of without worrying about whether they are good or bad."

The teacher describes the strategy: "Brainstorming helps you think about what you already know. You write down as many ideas as you can think of. You do not think about whether they are good or bad ideas while you do this. When you write down a lot of ideas, you may find some ideas that you didn't think about before. This is a good strategy to use when you don't have many ideas or when you aren't sure what you want to include in your writing."

The teacher models how to use the strategy, soliciting ideas from students: "I am going to show you how to brainstorm before writing a story on your topic. First, I will write down any idea that I think of about this topic. If I get stuck, I will keep thinking. I will not ask myself if an idea is a good one until I am done brainstorming. I will just write down any idea that pops into my head." *The teacher thinks aloud while modeling brainstorming, then asks:* "Does anyone else have any ideas to add to my list?"

Students collaborate in small groups to practice applying the strategy. The teacher explains: "I want each of you to pair up with another student. Before you start to write your story, the two of you should brainstorm as many ideas as you can for your paper on this topic. Remember not to worry about whether the ideas are good or bad. Right now, I just want you to focus on writing down as many ideas as you can." *While students practice using the strategy, the teacher checks to see that students are using the strategy properly and returns to earlier steps as needed.*

Students practice the strategy, with assistance from the teacher as needed. The teacher says: "Remember to brainstorm as many ideas as you can before you actually start writing your own paper." *While students generate their lists, the teacher walks around and assists students in applying the strategy.*

Students apply the strategy independently. The teacher reminds them: "Before you start to write, you should stop and ask if it will be helpful for you to use brainstorming to think about ideas for writing. Remember that brainstorming works well when you don't have many ideas or you aren't sure what you want to include in your writing." *If, in future lessons or on future topics, the teacher notices that students are having a hard time planning, he or she can remind students to use the brainstorming strategy.*

Adapted from Duke and Pearson (2002) in Shanahan, et al. (2010).

Note. From *Teaching Elementary School Students to Be Effective Writers: A Practice Guide* (p. 18) by S. Graham, A. Bollinger, C. Booth Olson, C. D'Aoust, C. MacArthur, D. McCutheon, and N. Olinghouse, 2012, Washington, D.C: National Center for Education and Evaluation and Regional Assistance, Institute of Education Sciences, U.S. Department of Education.

Although this graphic differs somewhat from the one depicted in Chapter Four, the same underlying notion of fostering increasing student responsibility for application of the knowledge or strategy over time is evident. Similarly, you can see critical phases of instruction. Too often, I see teachers start right out with modeling, or worse, guided practice, without the explicit explanation or description that many students need. Or I see teachers giving lots of explicit explanation or description but then turning students loose without the needed collaborative and guided practice. In the following two sections, I discuss some key practices you can use in specific phases of the gradual release.

MODELED WRITING, MENTOR TEXTS, AUTHOR STUDIES

We rely on models for nearly everything we do—in our parenting, we emulate people we think are good parents, in our work we emulate people who we think are exceptionally good at their jobs, and so on. Students rely on models too, and modeled writing, mentor texts, and author studies provide important models for them.

Modeled Writing

In modeled writing, the teacher writes a model text for students in, or partly in, their presence. Although the text may not have the same level of polish or quality as mentor texts or author studies, discussed later in this section, modeled writing enables students to see the process by which the text is composed, which is not possible with mentor texts or author studies (although author notes and videos are sometimes available to provide some insights into the author's process). For example, the teacher might demonstrate how she draws on her graphic organizer in composing her text or how she rereads the text looking for places that will provide additional detail.

Modeled writing often goes hand-in-hand with think-aloud. Think-aloud is when you say aloud what you're thinking as you engage in a process, and it appears to be a powerful instructional tool (Kucan & Beck, 1997). So much of what a good writer does is not visible by just watching the writer, and think-aloud helps make some invisible mental processes visible. For example, a teacher might think aloud about writing the beginning of an informative/explanatory article about spiders as follows:

> Okay, so I need to find a way to start my text. I could write, "This article is about spiders." That's true, but it's not a very exciting way to begin. I remember that the articles we have been looking at have interesting beginnings that make us want to read more. So let me think about some of the most interesting things I learned about spiders . . . Well, one thing I thought was really interesting is that most spiders have eight eyes! And I know that all spiders have eight legs. Maybe I can do something with that. Let's see . . . "What has eight eyes and eight legs? A monster? No! A spider!" I think that will get readers' attention and make them want to read more. When you are thinking about how to start your article, you can think about the most interesting things you have learned about your animal.

Notice that the think-aloud reveals a strategy that students can use in their own composition process: thinking about interesting things they learned about a topic to give them ideas about how to start the piece.

Often, it makes sense to model-write the same text over many sessions. For example, the teacher might continue this text on spiders by later model-writing the rest of the introduction (e.g., about what spiders are, different species, main points of the article), and then later the body of the article, the conclusion, the title, and the selection or creation of graphics, followed by revising, editing, and creating a final copy. Generally speaking, you should do your model-writing on a topic that is related to, but not the same as, the topic on which students are writing. For example, the teacher would model-write an article on spiders only if none of the students were writing texts on spiders. This helps prevent students from just copying what you've written. You should also be sure to model the challenges as well as the successes of writing. It is okay, in fact good, for students to see that sometimes you don't like what you wrote, sometimes you cross out and start over, sometimes you have a hard time thinking about how to word something, and so on. This is what real writing is like, and it will help validate students' own experiences if they see their teacher experiencing it as well.

Mentor Texts

For more on mentor texts refer back to pages 55–57. As noted there, mentor texts should be of the same genre and, if possible, the same format we want students to write. However, generally they should not be on the same topic, as students might then be tempted to copy or wonder why their text is needed. Mentor texts should provide high-quality writing that is reasonably accessible to children of that age. Pages 140–143 contain excerpts of mentor texts in some of the target genres discussed in this book.

A teacher reads a mentor text on surviving household dangers as a model of informative/explanatory writing for a unit on surviving dangers in the wild.

Informative/Explanatory: These pages are from Beachcombing: Exploring the Seashore by Jim Arnosky (2004).

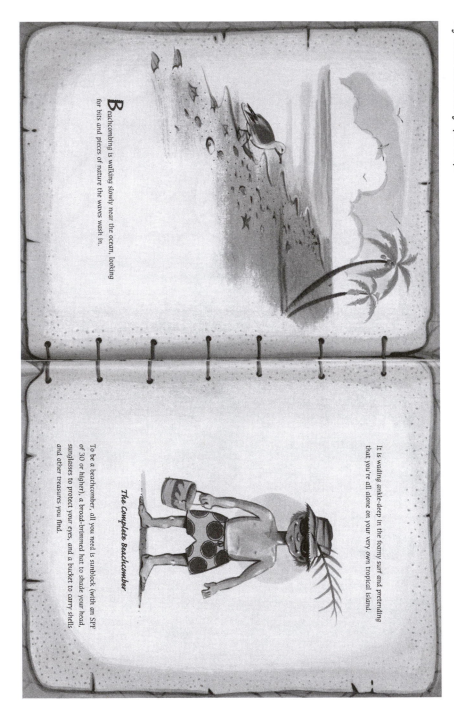

Beachcombing is walking slowly near the ocean, looking for bits and pieces of nature the waves wash in.

It is wading ankle-deep in the foamy surf and pretending that you're all alone on your very own tropical island.

The Complete Beachcomber

To be a beachcomber, all you need is sunblock (with an SPF of 30 or higher), a broad-brimmed hat to shade your head, sunglasses to protect your eyes, and a bucket to carry shells and other treasures you find.

Persuasive: These are the first two pages of "Gum Should Be Allowed at School" from "If You Want My Opinion . . .": Letters by Kids on Issues That Matter to Kids, edited by Raymond Coutu (2014).

Gum Should Be Allowed at School

By Anonymous, Waterboro, Maine

"Abby...." said the teacher.

"Yes."

"What are you eating?"

"Gum..."

"Go spit it out."

"Oh My Gosh... Fine."

"Don't do it again, it's disruptive."

Is that what happens to you? Well, I know this happens to me, and I am sick of it. It is time we protest.

How Gum Helps Kids

Do you get bored in class, or do you find you can't concentrate during the big science exam? Research has

shown that chewing gum in school can improve concentration and make it easier to pay attention. It can also help relieve stress from tests, projects, and homework. Some of the health benefits of chewing gum

are that it freshens breath, but better yet it increases saliva, which helps defend your teeth against plaque and other dental disease, such as cavities. This would help out families because with no cavities comes fewer dentist visits, which saves the family money. There would also be less time and pain spent on filling cavities. I don't know about you, but I would like to live a cavity-free life.

Another big reason is that chewing gum is cheap, low in calories, and fits in your pocket for easy management. At about 10 calories per piece, it is a good way

to keep children from snacking and may help the rate of obesity in kids decrease.

Now, don't get me wrong. Students sometimes do not dispose of their gum correctly. However, the reason that kids stick gum under their tables is that they are afraid of getting into trouble if their teachers catch them chewing it. They also get embarrassed when they have to spit it out because they got caught. But if students could chew gum and not have to hide it, they would probably dispose of it properly.

Biography: These pages—featuring Josephine Cochran, who invented an automatic dishwasher—are from *Inventors Who Have Changed Life at Home* by Sonia W. Black (2014).

Finally, Josephine's machine was ready. She used wire to form a dish rack. It had spaces to hold cups, saucers, and dishes in place. The rack sat inside a copper boiler with a motor. The motor spun a wheel at the bottom of the boiler. Then water jets pumped hot, soapy water to wash everything inside. The machine could wash 200 dishes in two minutes!

In 1886, Josephine received a patent for her great invention. She named it the Cochran Dishwasher. Then she formed the Garis-Cochran Dish-Washing Machine Company to make and sell the appliance. She advertised the machine in local newspapers, too. When she showed it at the 1893 Chicago World's Fair, it won an award for its design.

The 1886 patent for Josephine's invention shows the complicated dishwasher design.

The price of the Cochran Dishwasher was $250. That was expensive at the time. Most people could not afford to have one in their home. Most homes did not have the proper plumbing. They did not have hot water heaters big enough to run these new machines. So mostly restaurants and hotels bought them in the beginning. Some of Josephine's wealthy friends bought them, too.

Most families could not afford the Cochran Dishwasher, or early models like the one shown here.

Fun Fact

Josephine's dishwasher was not the first one invented. From the 1850s, other men and women inventors had received patents for similar machines. But Josephine's dishwasher was the most like today's electric dishwashers. It was the best of all at washing dishes.

22

Procedural: These are the first pages from an investigation in Gross Science! by Kristin Geller (2014).

A Fungus Among Us

Materials

- a pair of disposable gloves
- 3 slices of white bread (without preservatives is best)
- 3 plastic bags
- masking tape
- marker
- spray bottle filled with water

Do this investigation with an adult. When you're finished, remove your gloves carefully, place them in the garbage, and wash your hands.

Steps

1. Put on the gloves. Find three areas of a room that look dirty (floors, carpets, corners of the room) or are touched by many people (pencils, doorknobs, desks, tables).

2. Gently rub each of the three bread slices along a different dirty spot.

3. Carefully place each slice of bread inside a plastic bag. Mark the three bags, noting where you rubbed each slice.

7

4. Spray water inside each bag and onto the bread. (Make sure not to touch the bread with your hands.) Seal the bags.

5. Place the bags in a warm location without direct sunlight.

6. After a few days, your mold garden will grow!

8

Often teachers use just one mentor text, but sometimes it is useful to provide sets of mentor texts so students can see similarities across them.

Author Studies

Author studies are like mentor texts on steroids. With author studies, students have a whole collection of work to study, all by the same author (and, typically, of the same genre). They learn about the author's style and, often, about the author's life and his or her writing process. I have long been disappointed that author studies typically don't focus on authors of informational text, despite the existence of many authors worthy of such study (e.g., Duke & Bennett-Armistead, 2003).

You may be wondering how author studies fit into a project-based approach. Simply studying an author does not constitute a project that meets the criteria outlined in Chapter One. Rather, the author's work needs to be the springboard for a specific writing purpose and audience. For example, a study of Jeanette Winter's or Pam Muñoz Ryan's work—which often focuses on people or events that have made a difference in the world—might give rise to a project in which students write about other people who or events that have made a difference and/or a project in which students work to make a difference themselves. A study of the work of prolific children's informative/explanatory magazine writer Sara Goudarzi might give rise to a project in which students develop their own informative/explanatory magazine on a topic—such as animals—on which Goudarzi often writes.

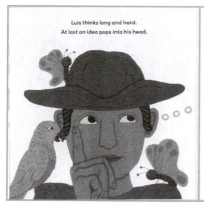

Luis thinks long and hard.
At last an idea pops into his head.

"I can bring my books into the faraway hills
to share with those who have none.

One burro could carry books,
and another burro could carry me—and more books!"

Jeanette Winter is one author of informational text whose work is worthy of study. This is an excerpt from her book *Biblioburro: A True Story from Colombia* (2010).

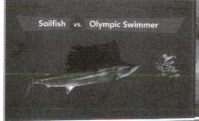

Sailfish   vs.   Olympic Swimmer

Named for the large sail-like fin on their backs, sailfish are the fastest swimmers around! They can shoot through the water at top speed.

The sailfish's super speeds come from its strong, streamlined body. Special grooves allow the fish to draw in its fins, making its body sleek and smooth. With features like this, sailfish beat out our top human swimmers any day.

By wearing a swim cap, Michael Phelps tries to streamline his body to increase his speed. Sailfish are naturally streamlined for speed.

Want to put it to the test? American gold medalist Michael Phelps swims the 200-meter freestyle in 1.42 minutes or 85.20 seconds. The sailfish could swim the same distance in 13 seconds! Even the record-holding Phelps isn't competition for the sailfish.

20

21

Sara Goudarzi is a children's magazine author whose work is also worthy of study. This is an excerpt from her article "Olympians vs. Animals" (2014).

Pam Muñoz Ryan has published acclaimed literary and informational texts. This is an excerpt from the largely nonfiction narrative text, *When Marian Sang: The True Recital of Marian Anderson, the Voice of a Century* (2002).

INTERACTIVE WRITING AND SCAFFOLDED WRITING

In reading, we can use a variety of strategies to support children in accessing text that they could not access on their own, such as reading the text aloud to them, reading the text with them (e.g., chorally or taking turns reading), and coaching them as they read. Similarly, there are strategies available to help children write text that they could not write on their own. In this section, I briefly discuss two such strategies: interactive writing and scaffolded writing.

Interactive Writing

Interactive writing involves children in contributing to a piece of writing. It is synonymous with or similar to (depending on whose description you read) shared writing or "sharing the pen." Research indicates that interactive writing fosters several areas of literacy development (Craig, 2003; Roth & Guinee, 2011). In Kate Roth and Kathleen Guinee's study, three first-grade teachers did interactive writing with students an average of 10.5 minutes each day, whereas three other teachers chose not to use this approach. Students in the interactive writing classrooms showed greater growth in writing independently and on nine of ten aspects of writing that align closely with important traits of writing (Culham, 2003): Ideas, Organization, Word Choice, Sentence Fluency, Spelling of High-Frequency Words, Spelling of Other Words, Capitalization, Punctuation, and Handwriting. Roth and Guinee provide a description from an interactive writing session they observed as part of a research study.

> Ms. Brown sits next to an easel in front of her first-grade class and prepares to help the students write another page in a class book about the seasons, an extension of their science unit on weather. 'We're writing about summer, and it's the coldest day of the year! That's a little strange. But I was thinking that if we're writing about all the things we do in summer, today, we can just close our eyes and pretend it is . . .'
>
> 'Summer!' shout the students.
>
> Together, the class rereads the previous pages in their big book. Then, they begin to brainstorm what to write next.

'In the summer we go swimming!' suggests Kaitlyn.

'We go to camp!' offers Dillon. The teacher reminds the students to think of things that are unique to the summer season and are relevant to everyone in the class, not just a few families.

After many children proposed activities, Ms. Brown asks, 'How can we put these ideas together so they would make sense?'

Jadana suggests writing 'In the summer we have vacation and can go to camp and to the beach, the pool, Canabe Lake Park, and Water Country.'

Ms. Brown guides the class as they divide these ideas into two sentences. She also models using words succinctly to summarize many ideas. 'What if we say amusement parks? That covers Canabe Lake and Water Country.'

The students repeat the two sentences a few times to 'make sure they sound right to our ears' and to count the number of words they will write.

Alyssa goes to the easel and quickly writes 'In the' on mounted sentence strips. While she does this, the whole class writes 'In the' with their fingers in the air to practice writing these high frequency words.

'Why did you write a capital I?' Ms. Brown asks. Alyssa explains she knew it was the first letter in a sentence. Then, she points to the words on the easel and leads the class in reading what they have written so far.

'Let's say the next word "summer" together slowly' suggests Ms. Brown.

Christopher goes to the easel and writes the letter 's'. The class then claps the first beat of the word and listens for the vowel sound.

'It's like the sound in "fun" ' suggests David.

Christopher continues to write the letters of summer as the class says the word slowly listening for each sound. 'The last sound is easy' boasts Christopher. The other students know that Christopher is the 'er' expert because of the 'er' at the end of his name.

The class continues to encode the message as the teacher helps them think about conventions of print, spelling, and handwriting.

After writing their message, the class revisits the text for a minute. Ms. Brown chooses students to come up to the easel to answer questions that help the class focus on the details of print. 'Who can come up and find a two syllable word?' 'How many sentences did we write?' 'What word ends the same as Christopher?' (Roth & Guinee, 2011, pp. 333–334)

Interactive writing can be carried out in a whole-class format, but it often makes sense to do it in a small-group setting with those students who need this additional level of support and so that each student can contribute more. In a project-based context, interactive writing should serve the project. The project's final product might be produced through interactive writing for all or a subset of students, although creating conditions in which students can produce "their own" writing for part of the project is often better. Pieces leading up to the project—for example, an introductory letter to the target audience or signs or labels used for celebration and presentation—can be produced using interactive writing.

Scaffolded Writing

Scaffolded writing is a technique for supporting writers that is usually used one-on-one. Originally developed by Elena Bodrova and Deborah J. Leong (1998), in brief, scaffolded writing involves the following:

1. The child orally composes, with assistance as needed, a short text (e.g., "a cloud" "Wangari planted trees.").

2. The teacher draws a line or uses a highlighter to mark a place for each word as he or she says each word aloud (eventually, the child does this himself or herself). The length of the lines corresponds roughly to the length of the words.

3. The teacher and child repeat the message, pointing to each space/word/mark. Over time, the teacher speaks in a lower voice so the child is doing the primary voicing of the words.

4. The child, with assistance as needed, writes each word or part of the word or a mark that represents the word on each line.

5. The child and the teacher read the completed text together.

Children in the very early stages of writing development might write just a scribble or letter-like shape on each line. Later, they might be able to write the first letter for each word, as in:

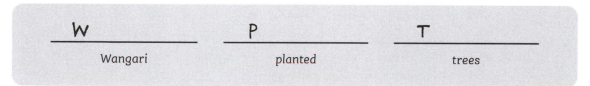

In time, students may capture multiple sounds within a given word, perhaps writing some words conventionally while estimating the spelling of others. In a project-based context, scaffolded writing might be used to enable some students who otherwise couldn't make or contribute to a final product for the project. For example, if the project involves making a class book, some children's pages could be produced using scaffolded writing, whereas others might be produced with less intensive support. You can download "Scaffolded Writing" by Deborah A. Rowe (2011), a very helpful article on varying the amount of support in scaffolded writing depending upon the child's developmental level. Go to https://sites.google.com/site/deborahwellsrowe/home and click on "Resources for Educators: Teachers and Coaches."

ASSESSMENT AND NEEDS-BASED GROUPING

The meta-analysis referenced earlier found that assessment was another intervention with positive effects on students' writing (Graham et al., 2012). In a project-based approach, we can glean valuable insights about students' development of 21st century skills (see pages 12–13), such as how they collaborate, problem solve, learn, and perform in a context (see http://www.edutopia.org for resources related to assessment in project-based contexts). However, projects typically do not allow us to see how students become completely independent writers. For that, I suggest using prompts before and/or after a unit to elicit writing along with rubrics to score that writing.

Example prompts appear below and example rubrics appear on page 152 (see Culham, 2003, for a discussion of traits of writing). The feedback and editing forms described in Chapter Six also provide valuable assessment tools, although again in a supported rather than an independent writing context.

PROMPTS FOR ELICITING INDEPENDENT WRITING SAMPLES

Your prompts for eliciting independent writing samples will depend on what you are trying to assess and the time you have available. For example, if you want to assess students' research skills as well as their writing, you will want a prompt that engages them in carrying out some research with sources you make available, whereas if you are less interested in this or have limited time, you will want to have them write on topics on which they are already knowledgeable. In any case, establishing an actual purpose and audience for the writing is likely to result in better quality writing (Block, 2013). Below is an example prompt for informative/explanatory writing (modeled after one developed by Debi Khasnabis, Cathy Reischl, and me):

This is a photo of _____ **[audience for writing—should be a real person]**. *She/he is* _____ **[give age if a child, explain role if a librarian or adult friend of yours or the like]**. *Take a good look at* _____ **[hold up photo of audience]**. _____ **[audience for writing]** *is very interested in learning about* _____ **[choose a topic on which you know your students have considerable knowledge, such as animals]**.

Now provide further information about the topic that will increase the chances the prompt elicits informative/explanatory text and not a story or some other text type. For example, for a text about animals, you might say: *"She/he wants to learn about all kinds of animals. Today, we'd like you to choose a kind of animal that you know a lot about. We would like you to write a short book with information about the kind of animal you choose.* _____ **[name of audience]** *will learn about the kind of animal you've written about when she/he reads your book."*

Prompts for other genres can be structured similarly, but emphasizing the purpose for that type of text:

Persuasive: prompt identifying a real audience that could realistically be persuaded or convinced of something

Nonfiction narrative: prompt identifying a real audience that would be interested in learning about a true event about which students have learned (or, to elicit personal narrative, in their own lives)

Biography: prompt identifying a real audience that would be interested in learning about a person about whom students are knowledgeable

Procedural: prompt identifying a real audience that needs or wants to learn how to do something that the audience doesn't know how to do and your students do know how to do

Giving students' samples back to them on a second day for revision and editing will allow you to examine their skills in that area as well. You may find you want to score the initial draft and then do a second score after revising and editing.

Once you have assessment data, whether from within the project or from prompted samples collected before the project, the needs-based grouping approach described on pages 106–107 kicks in again. You pull together students with similar needs for targeted instruction. I realize that one-on-one conferences are popular, and certainly there are times when they are appropriate, but I sometimes find that they are inefficient. When I see the teacher needing to say the same thing to multiple students, I wonder whether it might have been more efficient to pull students together in a group for that instruction. Similarly, students sometimes become more thoughtful and "meta-" about their writing in the presence of fellow students who are reflecting on their own writing than they are in just a one-on-one situation with the teacher.

WRITING CHECKLISTS AND RUBRICS

In Chapter Six, you will learn about writing checklists as a versatile and easy-to-use tool for assessing student writing. However, for more formal writing assessment, you may wish to use rubrics. Rubrics should be aligned to your instructional goals and specific grade level. For example, the following is a simple rubric designed to assess the CCSS expectations for informative/explanatory writing at grade 1:

0	1	2	3	4	5
Does not write anything	Does not demonstrate approaching meeting standard	Some limited movement toward meeting standard	Considerable movement toward meeting standard	Meets standard	Meets second-grade standard
		• names topic **OR** • supplies very limited facts about topic	• names topic **AND/OR** • provides some sense of closure **AND TO SOME EXTENT** • supplies facts about topic	• names topic • provides some sense of closure **AND CLEARLY** • supplies facts about topic	• writes informative/ explanatory texts in which they introduce a topic, use facts **and definitions** to develop points, and provide a **concluding statement or section**. (vs. "some sense of closure")

(Based on a rubric developed by Nell K. Duke, Kristine Schutz, Shana Rochester, and Hye Jin Hwang.)

You can use similar overarching categories to create rubrics for any grade level and the CCSS.

WHAT DO STUDENTS DO WHEN THEY ARE WAITING FOR MY SUPPORT? CENTERS!

Ideally, when you are working with an individual, a pair, or small group, the other students are busy working on their own writing and research. However, sometimes—most commonly in kindergarten and first grade and in classrooms with large numbers of students and few adult helpers—this is not the reality. In these situations, you don't want students to be sitting and doing nothing while they wait for your support. (Techniques for students to use to signal that they need your support appear on pages 72–73.) Centers can help you avoid that situation. Each center focuses on a writing activity—preferably related to the project but it may sometimes be a separate task—that students can engage in while they wait for your support. Generally, writing centers should also be held to the expectation of having a real purpose and audience for students' writing (an exception might be a center in which students work on handwriting or typing or play a computer game that reinforces knowledge or a particular skill). Examples of writing centers that might go with a project include the following:

- Helping to write a cover letter to accompany the texts that will be delivered to the audience

- Searching and collecting images that peers might choose among for their texts

- Listening to (at a listening center) or reading texts to deepen knowledge or understanding of content related to the project

- Listening to (at a Listening Center) or rereading mentor texts from the project

- Writing an e-mail or paper note to a family member updating him or her about the project

Centers not directly tied to the project that might be educative for students include:

- **Listening Center:** Students listen to audio-recordings of texts; be sure to include informational texts, even if you have to record them yourself or ask a volunteer to do so.

- **Reading Center:** Students read texts of their choice, preferably from a set selected by you based on their interests, background knowledge, and approximate reading level.

- **Computer Center:** Students engage with reading- or writing-related apps (see *Children's Technology Review* for ideas: http://www.childrenstech.com).

- **Letter Center:** Students write to friends, family, pen pals, or others (remember: pencil to paper, fingers to keys). You can also encourage them to write compliments for classmates, school staff, or others. Display copies of completed student work for which other students can compose compliments.

- **Review Center:** Students are provided with a template to use to write reviews of books, magazine articles, movies, restaurants, video games, or other things that people review. Depending on the grade level, this template may include the name of the material being reviewed, the name of the reviewer, an attention-grabbing introduction, a summary of the material, and a response/reaction to the material. Depending on the grade level, this may be as simple as a few words and a rating such as the one shown below.

Or it may be more complex, including opinion, reasons, facts and details, and concluding statement. Critical, of course, is that students share their reviews with other students (that is, the reviews have a true audience and purpose).

The key is to make sure that whatever we make available to students in centers is worthy of their time and does not become too much of a distraction from the project itself.

SMART SUPPORT

As noted in Chapter Four, a major factor that determines the success of a project is the degree to which the teacher provides each student with the support he or she needs to engage with and complete the project successfully. The following are K–2 support strategies designed for three populations: (1) students who need additional support, (2) students who need additional challenge, and (3) dual language learners.

Again, some of these K–2 examples come directly from research, others are based on our classroom experiences. I want to particularly acknowledge Estanislado S. Barrera, IV, Raymond Coutu, Ellen Daugherty Durr, Sarah Glasscock, Jean Lawler, and Tammi Van Buren for their contributions to this list.

For Additional Support

- Provide sentence starters or key words and phrases with picture clues on an anchor chart to help students get started with their writing.

- Help, or enlist volunteers to help, students by sitting beside them as they work, assisting them with letter formation, putting spaces between words, and so on. Or, gather a few students who aren't ready to work independently and do the task as a scaffolded writing activity.

- Assist students by using the dictation feature on a word processing program (or a classroom volunteer) to help them with the flow of ideas. From there, they can revise and edit the text.

- Support students' estimated spelling efforts by reminding them to stretch out words they are writing and listen for the sounds. You can write conventionally in a smaller size above the child's writing so it is legible to others.

- Assist students with illustrations by finding photos of and related to their subject and inviting them to use those photos as models for their drawing.

- Have students take photos or video of themselves or others doing a procedure to help them describe steps in a procedural text.

- Pull together a small group to provide extra support.

For Additional Challenge

- When students create a procedural text for a project, encourage them to read the procedure aloud to a group. They might also write about how this procedural text could be adjusted to apply to other topics or tasks. Ask them to think about questions such as, "Would I need the same materials?" "Would any of the steps change?" "How would they change?"

- Encourage students to work on adding more letter sounds to their words. They can work with a partner to brainstorm content for sections of the text.

- Ask students to write a two- or three-word title. Explain that short titles are powerful, too. Confer with students to draw out what they want to say. Or, work with a small group on scaffolded writing as necessary.

- When students create a persuasive text for their project, challenge them to look for additional reasons for their opinion and support those reasons with evidence from a wider variety or resources.

- Tell students to reread their work as they go, looking for missing details. They may add examples and comparisons, or a more engaging introduction.

Reaching Dual Language Learners

- Pair students who speak the same first language so they can translate for each other. Consider having students act out any action verbs.

- Co-construct with students a title and cover illustration. For a title, brainstorm key words that relate to the topic, and use them to create a lively title. For an illustration, ask students to tell you in their own words the best way to express the topic visually, and then have them draw based on what they say.

- If the project involves the creation of a persuasive text, pull together a group of students working on the same or a similar opinion. Encourage them to share reasons for their opinions and then help one another come up with explanations for why those reasons are important.

- Show students how to use Excel or similar software to generate a graphical representation of the data, such as pie charts and bar graphs.

- For additional research that might be needed in this phase, make additional photos and/or videos about the topic available to help students visualize. Include resources in students' home language when possible.

As with the strategies recommended for the Reading and Research phase, these strategies will not apply to every project and every learner. And again, I highly recommend that teachers of adjoining grade levels meet at the end of the year to share knowledge about what worked for specific learners and how students are progressing in moving toward independence with challenges and opportunities that project-based instruction brings.

Concluding Thoughts: Stepping Out of Your Comfort Zone

If you've been doing a writers' workshop and/or units of study for a while, you may be feeling overwhelmed about trying an approach to instruction with so many new elements. If so, please recall my request in Chapter One: Just try one project and see how it goes. Remember to keep in mind that the first time doing something is often the hardest. I hope your first go at a project-based unit to develop informational reading and writing will encourage you to do another—to make project-based instruction part of your teaching repertoire.

CHAPTER SIX The Revision and Editing Phase

Once students have a draft of their final product, the project enters the Revision and Editing phase. In this chapter, I share two overarching principles for guiding students in revision and editing: using multiple strategies and making feedback genre- and unit-specific.

Use Multiple Strategies

It can be difficult to get students, especially young students, to engage in meaningful revision. You can use a number of strategies to make it more manageable and satisfying for students of all ages.

Remind students of their purpose and audience frequently. Recall Meghan K. Block's (2013) study described in Chapter Two: Students engaged in more mechanical (e.g., spelling, punctuation) and content-oriented revisions when they had a specified purpose for writing. Consider talking explicitly about the effect that revision and editing could have on the audience, or in achieving the purpose, if the writing (or video or other text) is or is not well organized, clear, and mechanically sound. Students are more likely to revise and edit if they understand the consequences of not doing so.

Model and explicitly teach revision and editing. For any process that is new to them, students need to see how it is done. Let them watch as you revise and edit a piece of writing on chart paper or a projector. You can use your own writing, which should match the genre students are writing, or a student's writing. If you use a student's writing, I recommend using pieces from previous years or by students from other classes—without the writers' names on them—so students in your class feel comfortable and don't have all the revising and editing done for them by you. Don't overwhelm students by demonstrating too many kinds of revisions at once. Align the revisions you demonstrate to the instructional goals you have set for the session.

Be specific. I have come to understand from research that feedback such as "Good job" or "That's coming along" is not very helpful, and potentially even harmful, to students. Instead, we need to identify for the student specifically what makes something a good job as in:

> "I like the way you started that paragraph—it tells what the whole paragraph is about."

> "I like the way you're using humor. It seems right for the audience."

> "I like all the precise vocabulary you're using. It helps me 'see' what you're saying."

> "I like the way you spelled that word—I can really see you were listening to the sounds in the word."

Don't have students revise and edit everything at once. A problem I'm guilty of in my own teaching of adults is to cover their papers with comments on everything from proper italicization to the structure of a section to the interpretation of a specific research study. Research, cognitive load theory, and just common sense suggest that this is not the way to go for adults, and it certainly seems not the way to go for children either. By looking at so many aspects of the writing at once, I am likely to miss things, and the feedback can be overwhelming for the writers. Instead, have students read through their own and their peer's text multiple times, each time with a particular focus. You will see later in this chapter that I provide separate checklists for revision and for editing, and even within these categories I suggest multiple read-throughs with different foci.

Construct whole-class lessons to focus on areas in which many students need to revise. When I plan a project-based unit for supporting informational reading and writing development, I like to leave some lessons open to be filled in later so that I can address specific issues I see arising in students' writing. (Even experienced teachers cannot always predict these issues.) When you teach such a lesson, make time that day for students to make revisions based on what you just taught.

Consider pulling small groups together to address specific writing issues. Oh, if only all students had the same issues to address in their writing! Given that reality is not that simple, it may make a lot of sense during small-group, partner, and individual work time to pull together students who have the same writing issue—in other words to differentiate instruction. For example, a student who is already using periods correctly does not have to sit through a lesson on that topic, and a student still working on this does not have to be overwhelmed or confused by a lesson on semicolons.

Praise revision. During whole-class wrap-ups during the Revision and Editing phase, call out examples of good revisions that specific students made. This will help convey to students that revision is valued, as well as giving them concrete examples of revisions to apply to their own work.

Use peers. There is some research to support having students exchange feedback with peers as a way to develop their revision and editing skills. (See discussion in Graham et al., 2012.) However, research-supported approaches and my own experiences suggest that peer feedback needs to be structured more than it typically is. The predicable "I like your writing" and "Maybe you could add more details . . ." aren't sufficiently specific or helpful. You'll see examples later in this chapter of peer feedback forms that help bring focus and specificity to feedback.

Recruit representatives of the target audience. When adult writers seek feedback on their writing, they often look to members of their target audience or people similar to them. For example, I should ask teachers and educational leaders for feedback on a draft of this book, and cookbook authors often ask potential users of their cookbook to try the recipes. When possible (and I understand that logistically it just isn't always possible), invite representatives of the target audience to complete feedback forms or confer with students about their writing. For example, if students are writing persuasive flyers on an upcoming ballot question, ask a friend who is a potential voter to come in and give feedback. Of course, you don't want to diminish the impact of the final product by having everyone in your target audience provide feedback on the draft. In some cases you may need to approximate the audience. For example, if students are writing a classroom pet and plant care guide for their kindergarten buddies, you might ask the kindergarten teacher to come in to provide feedback.

Establish a school-wide system of revision and editing marks and a plan for which ones will be taught at specific grade levels. One of the things I have seen hamper students' revisions and peer feedback is not having access to a set of marks for editing and revision or, perhaps worse, being taught a different set of marks every year. I encourage your school or even district to have a meeting, decide on a set of marks that everyone will use, and determine at which grade levels they will be taught. This should facilitate students' editing and revision development.

Insert a word or punctuation mark	⌃	Add a comma	⌄
Cut a word or words	ℓ	Start a new paragraph	¶
Move a word or words	→	Correct the spelling	sp. ◯
Add a period	⊙	Make a capital letter	≡

FIGURE 6.1: Sample editing marks chart. Download a full-size version of this chart at http://umich.edu/~nkduke/.

Teach students to use digital editing and commenting tools. Recall that the CCSS want students using digital tools to produce and publish writing beginning in kindergarten. This means that it is not enough to just teach editing and revision marks for use on paper, students also need to learn digital tools for editing and commenting. Again, it is ideal if the school or even district comes to agreement about the set of tools that students will use: Will they learn Google Docs' comment function? Microsoft® Word's? Other? In teaching these tools, try not to take anything for granted. You might know that a red squiggly underline in Microsoft Word suggests that a word may be misspelled, but do students know that? You might know that a green squiggly underline suggests a problem with grammar, but do students?

Use the standards. Digital editing tools may generate lots of red and green squiggly underlines, for spelling and grammar respectively, that students should not be expected to address. Students should only be expected to revise their writing to meet their grade level's standards, or not even that if it's early in the year and you haven't taught to some of those standards yet. (See especially the CCSS Language Standards, pages 26–29, which deal with capitalization, punctuation, and spelling, among other things.) This does not mean you as the teacher can't make corrections later. (See pages 174–175 for my recommendations on spelling for publication.) It just gives an indication of what students should be accountable for.

STAY AWAY FROM "DAILY ORAL LANGUAGE" AND EDITING WORKSHEETS

I am not aware of research showing that "daily oral language" or editing worksheets have a lasting, positive impact on students' writing. I also don't know of any colleagues who support these practices. In the What Works Clearinghouse *Practice Guide on Teaching Elementary School Students to Be Effective Writers*, the authors write, "Revising helps students apply their skills in authentic settings, as opposed to editing language on a generic worksheet" (Graham et al. 2012). This leads me to think that that panel also does not support editing worksheets or the like. Engaging students in editing their own and others' writing for a purpose and audience is likely to have a more positive impact on their writing.

Make Feedback Genre- and Unit-Specific

Recall from Chapter One, and throughout this book, that different kinds of text have different purposes and features that are read differently by proficient readers and written differently by proficient writers. Given this, it makes sense for feedback to be not generic but genre-specific (Duke, Caughlan, Juzwik, & Martin, 2012). For example, when I'm evaluating a nonfiction narrative, I'm looking for temporal terms and other signals to the timing of events. When I'm reading an informative/ explanatory text—with rare exceptions for some topics—I am not looking for these features. When I'm reading a persuasive text, I'm looking for reasons and evidence to support the opinion, but when I'm reading an informative/explanatory text, I often take the author's word for a point (assuming the author is credible) and am focused on learning about a topic rather than assessing the strength of an argument.

DECIDING ON THE FOCUS OF FEEDBACK

How do you decide on which points about a genre to look for?

- Look at CCSS Writing Standards 1 (opinion), 2 (informative/explanatory), or 3 (narrative), depending on what students are writing, for your grade level. Those genre-specific standards should probably be a focus of feedback.

- Refer to the other Writing standards as well as the Language standards for your grade level to identify other possible standards-aligned points for feedback.

- Revisit what you taught during the unit (and, if applicable, previous units). If you emphasized grabbing readers' attention, you should make that a point of feedback. If you didn't, you probably shouldn't include it. You can't ask students to give or receive feedback on every single aspect of writing of that genre; it makes sense to focus on those aspects you have worked on with them.

- Consider involving students in deciding on the focus of the feedback. What is most important to them, collectively or individually, about the writing in this project? What characteristics do they think are most important? What do they care most about? The meta-level nature of this kind of conversation may benefit students as writers, and they may work harder if they feel some ownership of the feedback questions.

STRUCTURING FEEDBACK

I believe, and there's some indication from research, that feedback works best when it is structured (Graham et al., 2012). On page 165, you'll find a feedback form template in which you can fill in points from the relevant standards and points you have taught in a unit in order to structure feedback on students' writing.

This template can be used for:

- Students' feedback on their own writing

- Peers' feedback on students' writing

- Your feedback on students' writing

- Representatives of the target audience's feedback on students' writing

Once you have completed a template, with the categories/foci for feedback, I suggest using it for both peer feedback and feedback from you. You might find that a different format for eliciting feedback makes sense for feedback from representatives of the target audience. For example, if your students are writing for preschoolers and they are receiving feedback from a preschool teacher, feedback might instead be structured with a series of questions such as:

What will preschoolers like about this book?

What could make this book more interesting for preschoolers?

What will be clear about this book for preschoolers?

How could the book be made clearer for preschoolers?

Students share and discuss their drafts with each other.

Feedback Form

Writer: _____   Reviewer: _____

	Yes	No. I suggest you try this:
	☐	
	☐	
	☐	
	☐	
	☐	
	☐	
	☐	

Something I especially like: _____

_____

A suggestion I have: _____

_____

A question I have: _____

FIGURE 6.2: Feedback form template. Download full-size versions of this form and the sample forms on pages 166–168 at http://umich.edu/~nkduke/.

Now let's look at how these feedback forms might be filled in for different genres and units:

Feedback Form

Writer: _____

Reviewer: _____

	Yes (✓)	No. I suggest you try this:
Does the title grab attention and tell what the booklet is about?	☐	
Does the introduction grab attention and tell what the booklet is about?	☐	
Does the booklet have information on each page organized around a specific topic or topics?	☐	
Does the booklet have connecting words, such as and, but, so, often, because?	☐	
Do the illustrations give information?	☐	
Does the conclusion explain threats to the animal and ways to help?	☐	

Something I really like about the writing: _____

Something I really like about the illustrations: _____

FIGURE 6.3: Sample grade 2 feedback form for informative/explanatory text

Feedback Form

Writer: _____

Reviewer: _____

	Yes (✓)	No. I suggest you try this:
Does the introduction clearly give an opinion?	☐	
Does the Core Democratic Value connect to the opinion?	☐	
Are the reasons for the opinion clear?	☐	
Are the reasons supported by data?	☐	
Do linking words connect opinions and ideas?	☐	
Does the conclusion restate the opinion?	☐	

Something I really like about the writing: _____

Something you might try: _____

FIGURE 6.4: Sample grade 2 feedback form for persuasive text

Feedback Form

Writer: _____

Reviewer: _____

	Yes (✓)	No. I suggest you try this:
Does the introduction grab the reader's attention?	☐	
Do the illustrations connect to the text?	☐	
Do the captions explain the illustrations?	☐	
Does the text teach facts about the inventor's life?	☐	
Does the text teach facts about the invention?	☐	
Is the book interesting to read?	☐	
Does the conclusion make the biography feel complete?	☐	
Does the index help readers find important information?	☐	

Something I really like about the writing: _____

Something you might try: _____

FIGURE 6.6: Sample grade 2 feedback form for biography

Feedback Form

Reviewer: _____

Writer: _____

	Yes (✓)
a capital letter?	☐
a plant or animal?	☐
detail?	☐
true information?	☐
Does it look like a Jeanette Winter page?	☐

☺ What I like most: _____

➕ Think about adding: _____

FIGURE 6.5: Sample kindergarten feedback form for nonfiction narrative

Feedback Form

Writer: _____

Reviewer: _____

	Yes (✓)	No. I suggest you try this:
Does the draft have a title that tells what the procedure is about?	☐	
Does the draft have all materials listed in order?	☐	
Does the draft have steps?	☐	
If so, are the steps clear and complete?	☐	
Does the draft have a "Why It Works" section?	☐	
If so, does the "Why It Works" section explain the science?	☐	
Does the illustration show the final product?	☐	

Something I really like about the writing: _____

Something you might try: _____

FIGURE 6.7: Sample grade 2 feedback form for procedural text

Partners each fill out a feedback form to make suggestions for revision.

Again, your own feedback forms may vary from these based on what you have taught during the unit and in previous units.

EDITING IS EDITING, REGARDLESS OF GENRE . . . USUALLY

Unlike most aspects of revision, editing is not very genre-specific: The rules of spelling, capitalization, and punctuation remain constant, almost regardless of the genre in which we are writing. For that reason, the form or approach you use for editing does not need to change from genre to genre, although it may be augmented from unit to unit as you give more lessons on mechanics.

On the following pages, I have included a sample editing checklist for each grade from K to 5. (Generally, I recommend using an editing checklist with kindergarten only toward the very end of the year.) The points in these checklists are aligned with the Language CCSS for each grade level. Please note that the standards are end-of-year goals, so you may not want to include all of these points on the checklist for units that are early in the year. Full-sized versions of these checklists can be downloaded at http://umich.edu/~nkduke/.

Editing Checklist

I have checked my message for:

☐ Capital letters →

☐ Punctuation

☐ Spelling

☐ Spaces between words →→

This checklist is based on CCSS expectations for kindergarten.

FIGURE 6.8: Sample kindergarten editing checklist

Editing Checklist

I have reviewed this article for:

Spelling

☐ spelled correctly words I have been taught

☐ used letter sounds to spell words I have not been taught

Capitalization

☐ capitalized the first word of each sentence

☐ capitalized dates and names of people

Punctuation

☐ used a period (.), question mark (?), or exclamation point (!) at the end of each sentence

☐ used commas (,) in dates and after words in a list

This checklist is based on CCSS expectations for end of grade 1.

Information taken from In by Nell K. Duke & Scholastic Inc.

FIGURE 6.9: Sample grade 1 editing checklist

Editing Checklist

I have reviewed this handout for:

Spelling

- ☐ spelled correctly words I've been taught
- ☐ used spelling patterns I know to spell words I've not been taught

Capitalization

- ☐ capitalized the first word of each sentence
- ☐ capitalized dates and names of people
- ☐ capitalized holidays, product names, and place names

Punctuation

- ☐ used a period (.), question mark (?), or exclamation point (!) at the end of each sentence
- ☐ used apostrophes (') in contractions and to show ownership
- ☐ used commas (,) in dates and after words in a list

This checklist is based on CCSS expectations for end grade 2.

FIGURE 6.10: Sample grade 2 editing checklist

Peer Editing Checklist

Writer: _____   Reviewer: _____

Spelling

- ☐ spelled correctly words we've been taught
- ☐ used spelling patterns to spell words we've not been taught

Capitalization

- ☐ capitalized holidays, product names, and place names
- ☐ capitalized titles of books, movies, and other works

Punctuation

- ☐ used commas in addresses (example: The White House, 1600 Pennsylvania Ave. NW, Washington, DC 20500)
- ☐ used commas in greetings and closings of letters (example: Best wishes, David)
- ☐ used commas and quotation marks for direct speech (example: "The sun is actually a star," she said.)
- ☐ used apostrophes to form contractions (example: He can't vote until he's 18.)
- ☐ used apostrophes to show ownership (example: Mercury's temperature can reach 800 degrees Fahrenheit!)

This checklist is based on CCSS expectations for grades 2 and 3.

FIGURE 6.11: Sample grade 3 editing checklist

Peer Editing Checklist

Writer: _____   Reviewer: _____

Spelling

☐ spelled correctly words we've been taught

☐ used spelling patterns to spell words we've not been taught

Capitalization

☐ capitalized titles of books, movies, and other works

☐ capitalized other words in all the right places

Punctuation

☐ used commas in addresses (example: The White House, 1600 Pennsylvania Ave. NW, Washington, DC 20500)

☐ used commas and quotation marks for direct speech and quotations from text (example: "The sun is actually a star," she said.)

☐ used commas in compound sentences (example: The Pilgrims first settled in Provincetown, but they moved on to Plymouth.)

☐ used apostrophes to show ownership (example: Mercury's temperature can reach 800 degrees Fahrenheit)

FIGURE 6.12: Sample grade 4 editing checklist

Peer Editing Checklist

Writer: _____   Reviewer: _____

Spelling

☐ spelled words for our grade correctly

Capitalization

☐ capitalized words in all the right places

Punctuation

☐ used punctuation to separate items in a list

☐ used underlining, quotation marks, or italics for titles of books, movies, and other works

☐ used commas to separate introductory statements from the rest of the sentence (example: Although many people fear sharks, most species are harmless to humans.)

☐ used commas to set off the words yes and no (example: Was the Declaration of Independence signed in 1776? Yes, it was.)

☐ used commas to set off tag questions from the rest of the sentence (example: Penguins live in Antarctica, don't they?)

☐ used commas to address someone (example: Welcome to our school, Mayor Martinez.)

☐ used commas and quotation marks for direct speech and quotations from text (example: "The sun is actually a star," she said.)

☐ used commas in compound sentences (example: The Pilgrims first settled in Provincetown, but they moved on to Plymouth.)

FIGURE 6.13: Sample grade 5 editing checklist

Students can use these checklists to review their own writing, and peers can use them to review one another's writing (although this may not be appropriate for kindergarten and early first grade). You will probably prefer to edit right on students' papers or in their electronic files, rather than using the editing checklist.

BEYOND FORMS AND CHECKLISTS

Most of us as adult writers do not use forms and checklists to guide our revision and editing. At some point, we want students to internalize the language of these tools so they don't rely on the tools themselves. As a step toward more self-regulated revision and editing, some scholars recommend teaching heuristics for students to keep in mind as they edit or revise. For example, you may have heard of "COPS," an acronym for capitalization, overall appearance or organization (depending on whose version you use), punctuation, and spelling (Schumaker et al., 1982). Research does not yet provide a clear answer as to when students are best positioned to move beyond forms and checklists; it may depend upon the complexity of the writing project itself and other factors. But it is a worthwhile topic for teachers within a school to discuss.

Concluding Thoughts: Revising Revision

It's safe to say, revision and editing is the step in the writing process that we—including myself—teach least well. So often we don't allocate enough time for revision or provide enough support. Or the support we do provide is too generic, too unstructured, and too haphazard. I hope this chapter has offered some tools you can use to support revision and editing development better. I hope project-based instruction provides you and your students with more motivation to engage in revision and editing. In the next chapter, I address a topic that is a lot of fun—the presentation and celebration of students' projects.

CHAPTER SEVEN The Presentation and Celebration Phase

The Presentation and Celebration phase occurs on the last day of a project-based unit, when the final product is complete and it is time to send or deliver it to its audience. Students, you, or another adult might take the product to the audience, the audience might come to students to receive it, or it might be sent to the audience using traditional mail or e-mail. However the final product is delivered, it is important to create ceremony around getting it to its audience. For example, in teacher Jen Drew's second-grade classroom at Jayno Adams Elementary School, in Waterford, Michigan, I watched as students put their finished booklets on endangered sea animals into a box for delivery, one by one, some of them giving their work a little kiss as they did so. This kind of ceremony reinforces the project purpose, product, and audience, and underscores the communicative function of composing.

Beyond the ceremony of getting the product to its audience, I have three points to make about the Presentation and Celebration phase: Make sure the product is audience-ready; obtain a response from the audience, if possible; and celebrate! I end the chapter with some enjoyable and effective ideas for celebrations.

Make Sure the Product Is Audience-Ready

If at all possible, students' work should go to the audience when it is ready, not by some predetermined schedule. Some students may need more time than planned to develop a strong product, and the stakes of many projects are high enough that they will likely want to develop a strong product.

Naturally, it is important for the audience to be able to read the final product. Although young children should be encouraged to use invented, estimated, or temporary spelling, I believe that a teacher or other adult should write the correct spelling in small print or type near students' unconventional attempts. This ensures that those who receive the writing, which may include people who are not practiced in reading young children's writing, can actually read it. Legibility is essential to the success of a project-based approach, in which so much emphasis is placed on communicating with an audience.

A student's "Why We Write" poster with teacher handwriting providing conventional spellings of words audience members might not otherwise be able to read.

Obtain a Response From the Audience, if Possible

Children, like adults, appreciate responses to what they create. These responses may be especially important for children because the feedback helps them to understand the communicative nature of writing, drawing, filming, and so forth; increases their awareness of audience; and reinforces their investment in composing. If children are delivering their product in person, they may receive an immediate response, though a follow-up as well is ideal. If they are delivering the product via traditional mail or e-mail, or if you are delivering it for them, a delayed response will need to be requested. If you inform audience members of the need for a response from the outset of a unit (see Chapter Three), it may be easier to get one from them at the end. If audience members do not come through with a response, you could even draft a potential response for them, in hopes that they will modify it to reflect their own thinking and send it back to you.

Sometimes, the response is really about whether the product that students have developed has the desired impact. For example, in the park improvement project described in Chapter Two, a key part of the response was whether the proposal would actually result in the city's making improvements to the park. In my experience, in some cases it does have the desired impact, and in some cases it does not. If it does, students receive a powerful message not only about the power of writing (and graphics and presentation) but also about the power of citizens. If it doesn't, students are disappointed, but you can help them deal with their disappointment. For example, a teacher may emphasize a city official's positive feedback on the proposal, factors that may make the proposal difficult to enact at that time (e.g., a troubled city's finances), and ways in which exercising your power as citizens can be powerful, even if things don't always go your way.

Celebrate!

Often, completing a project is something to celebrate in its own right. I recommend celebrations that are tightly linked to the project itself and, when possible, widen the audience in some way. Examples of possible celebrations for three projects appear below.

PROJECT 1: CLASSROOM JOBS MANUAL

Children write procedural texts about how to do various jobs in the classroom for new students and other students in the class who have not yet done that job.

Celebrating the Project

- Invite a buddy classroom to visit. Have students "host" the job about which they wrote by reading their page to a visitor and asking him or her to then try doing the job.

- Ask family members to preview and learn about jobs in the classroom.

- As an interactive writing activity, write a letter to future students, welcoming them, introducing the classroom jobs manual, and explaining how they might use it.

- Hold a "How-to Text Extravaganza!" Have a variety of procedural texts posted at centers so students can rotate and carry out each activity. It would be helpful to have parent volunteers at each center. Some centers might include:

  » A collection of other topics about which students could write a procedural text for the classroom, such as ordering a hot lunch, following dismissal procedures, using the listening center, and so on

  » A collection of simple procedural texts about arts and crafts that students could try doing, such as how to make a bookmark, how to use watercolor paints, and how to make a pencil holder (Or you might want to consider a collection about games and exercises.)

  » A collection of simple games with procedural texts that explain how to play them

Reaching the Audience

- Post pages at locations in the classroom where jobs are typically carried out. For example, the librarian page would be posted at a child's eye-level in the classroom library.

- Work with students in an interactive writing lesson to create a cover and table of contents for the jobs manual. Bind the book and put it in the classroom library for future job-doers.

PROJECT 2: LETTERS TO THE EDITOR OF A LOCAL NEWSPAPER OR ONLINE NEWS SITE

Students select issues of relevance to their community and write letters to the editor of a local newspaper or online news site expressing their opinion and supporting it with reasons.

Celebrating the Project

- Invite the publisher or an editor from a local newspaper or news website to your class to talk about his or her job, the process of newspaper publishing, and the role of letters to their readers. Present the visitor with your letters.

- Publish a classroom newspaper with a collection of all the letters for students to take home, in addition to sending them to the local newspaper or on-line source.

- Invite families to come to the classroom to preview the letters and learn about your research process. Display results from the survey and research materials.

- Celebrate the spirit of your students' topics. For example, if some of the letters that students wrote champion improving a community park, perhaps students and families can hold a "working bee" to kick off the effort.

Reaching the Audience

- Be sure to send the letters to the local news sources. Remember to come up with as many possible outlets as you can, in case the local newspaper or news website can't publish all of them. For example, try the town's online homepage, a neighborhood newsletter or newspaper, or a regional newspaper.

PROJECT 3: PROPOSALS TO CONSERVE A LOCAL ECOSYSTEM

Students study problems associated with a local ecosystem and create a proposal with possible solutions to present to their city council or town hall and other local community members.

Celebrating the Project

- Take another trip to the local ecosystem, this time having a picnic or other celebration while there.

- Invite people who have careers involving the environment to speak to your class about their field and experiences and to learn about students' proposals.

- Arrange for schoolmates to pair up with students from your classroom. Ask them to listen to their partner's presentation and provide feedback. When they are finished, give them a chance to go outside and enjoy their playground ecosystem.

- Hold a reception after the proposal is presented with food and drink related to the ecosystem. For example, if the proposal involves the wetlands, you or a volunteer might serve "Frogs on a Log" (olives and cream cheese on celery, as shown at the right).

Reaching the Audience

- If students are presenting the proposal at a public meeting, confirm those arrangements.

- If students are presenting the proposal in your classroom, consider sending out invitations not only to city council members and other local community members but also to a local newspaper or news site, families, and members of the school community.

Following Up With the Audience

- Consider polling the audience after the presentation for their opinions on conserving the local ecosystem.

- Pass out feedback sheets for audience members to fill out before they leave or send a link to an online survey.

Concluding Thoughts: Whew!

At this point, you've experienced, or at least read about, the project process from beginning to end. Congratulations! I hope you'll take a few minutes to relish your accomplishment before moving on to the next of the many things on your plate. I also hope that in reflecting on the project process, you find that you would like to carry out a unit if you haven't done so yet—or to continue to carry out more. That's where the next chapter comes in. It addresses strategies for making project-based instruction more professionally manageable.

CHAPTER EIGHT Making Project-Based Instruction Professionally Manageable

In Chapter Three, I talked about managing project-based instruction. This chapter is about making it manageable—in other words, giving you as a teacher ways to develop and implement projects as practically as possible. In terms of the time, effort, and thinking that go into it, project-based instruction is more challenging than some traditional forms of instruction, such as following a ready-made core reading program manual or carrying out writers' workshop basically the same way you've been doing for years. But there are ways to make project-based instruction manageable. In this chapter, I give you strategies for doing that.

Be Strategic About Your Project Load

You want to be able to create new projects every year, depending on that year's current events (as in the Hurricane Sandy Project in Chapter Three), specific problems, needs or occasions that arise, and that particular class's interests and assets. However, it may not be feasible, or even advisable, for every project you do in a year to be brand new. Some projects you develop can work every year. For example, you can reuse the classroom jobs manual project referenced earlier every year, as every year there will be a need (new students who come in during the year or students who have not yet done a particular classroom job) and the jobs themselves and ways of doing them may change. Every year students can make a guide to their grade for next year's class. Every year students can create a video yearbook recounting their year. And so on. (See the Class Newsletter box on the next page for another idea.) Reusing some projects several years in a row means that you aren't developing all new projects every year.

CLASS NEWSLETTER

A project that can work every year is a periodic class newsletter to families authored by groups of students. Students might take on particular departments, or "beats," and rotate them with each edition:

- Key concepts they are learning in their science and social studies instruction

- Special events in the classroom

- What's been happening in art, music, PE, and library

- Book reviews (a form of persuasive writing)

- Puzzles and trivia questions to answer

- Cartoons and other visual features

- Letters to readers (which could entail persuasive writing)

- And, of course, a description of the project the class is currently working on!

If possible, consider digitizing the newsletter for distribution to families' mobile devices. If some of your families are not literate in English, try to find someone who would be willing to take on the task of translating the newsletter into families' home languages.

If you are in project-based instruction for the long haul, then you can also rotate projects year to year. For example, if you have a project that involves studying and documenting living things around the school to present to the PTO members and/ or neighbors or conservation groups, you might carry it out every few years rather than every year. If students recall that their older siblings, cousins, or friends did the project, you can explain that the living things might have changed—and, in fact, knowing whether or not they have changed may be valuable. In sum, I encourage you to look across the school year and manage your project load, with not too many, or too few, new projects to offer.

Share Projects

Another way to make project-based instruction more professionally manageable is to share projects among a group of teachers. For example, if there are three fourth-grade teachers in your school, and each of you writes a unit, that makes three units that can be taught to fourth graders in the school that year (assuming they are projects that lend themselves to being carried out by such a large number of fourth graders). You can also, or instead, share projects across schools. For example, if you know a colleague who teaches the same grade level at a different school in the district, you could arrange to swap units so that you each write one but have two available to teach.

Getting your district's curriculum coordinators, if you have them, on board with project-based instruction can also be a major support. They might be willing to allocate some district resources to developing project-based units. For a particularly powerful combination, try to get the literacy coordinator to collaborate with the social studies and/or science coordinators in the district, so that project-based units can be developed that address both literacy and science and/or social studies goals. If the science coordinator expresses concern about integrating literacy with science, you can reassure him or her that research clearly shows that students learn more science when text and hands-on experiences are combined, rather than when hands-on experiences are taught alone (e.g., Anderson, 1998; Cervetti, Barber, Dorph, Pearson, & Goldschmidt, 2012). Although comparative studies like these have not been carried out in social studies, related studies suggest the promise of instruction that combines literacy and social studies instructional goals (see Monte-Sano, 2012, for an introduction to this work).

Some project-based purists would say that implementing a unit that someone else has designed is inconsistent with the fundamental ideals of project-based instruction— that the projects need to come from that specific classroom context and from the students in that context. I do not hold that position. Recall my description of project-based approaches from Chapter One:

> In a project-based approach, students work over an extended time period for a purpose beyond satisfying a school requirement—to build something, to create

something, to address a question they have, to solve a real problem, or to address a real need.

Based on that description, shared units can still constitute project-based instruction. That said, you can keep yourself honest by looking at any potential project with a critical eye: *Does this project involve the kind of purpose, final product, and audience I want to embrace? Is it well aligned with my instructional goals? Will it be engaging to my students?* When you are implementing a project designed by someone else, you should be especially diligent about assessing its launch (see pages 61–62) and monitoring students' understanding of and engagement in the project purpose throughout. Finally, you don't have to implement a shared project to the letter. You may be able to adjust and adapt it to better fit your students and goals.

TEACHING OTHER EDUCATORS' PROJECT-BASED UNITS AS A FORM OF PROFESSIONAL DEVELOPMENT

Another argument for teaching some project-based units designed by curriculum coordinators, colleagues, or others is that the experience might help further your ability to design and implement your own units. In fact, I had just that in mind when a team of consultants, editors, and I developed a set of project-based units, part of a product called *Information in Action*, for grades K–5. At each grade level, one unit focuses primarily on persuasive text, one on informative/explanatory text, one on procedural text, and one on either biography or nonfiction narrative. Our hope is not for teachers to use these units forever, but to try them out, adjust and adapt them, and go on to design and implement their own units.

Collaborate Around Project Development

A final strategy is to actually develop project-based units collaboratively. A Professional Learning Community, or PLC, would be an excellent forum for this kind of work. Sharon Walpole and Kristina Najera (2013) recently reviewed research on collaborations for school-wide instruction in reading. They found that true collaboration typically requires a cultural shift and considerable time and resources.

When it's working effectively, collaboration proceeds in stages, from building community, to grappling with ideas, to finding common ground, to applying ideas, and eventually to establishing new goals (p. 514). Walpole and Najera provide a template for planning collaboration, below and on the next page, that is well suited to

PLANNING TEMPLATE FOR COLLABORATION

Set a goal and vision.

All members of a collaborative team must know why they are working together and what they hope to accomplish.

What is our goal?

Choose the right team.

If the goal of a collaboration affects others, they must be included on the team from the beginning. Having their input as decisions are made is much more productive than gathering it afterward.

Who should be here?

Gather resources before you start.

Time, money, space, books, data, or personnel resources essential to the collaboration must be acquired up front. It does not make sense to meet without adequate tools.

What do we need?

(continued)

FIGURE 8.1: Planning template for collaboration from Walpole and Najera (2013, pp. 517–518), based on Mohammad et al. (2011)

collaboration around project-based unit development. They also provide helpful advice about how to support collaboration at the district level (See Figure 8.2 on page 186). Project-based unit design is a sufficiently complex process that I encourage you to use these tools when you develop units with your colleagues.

Think about constructive, respectful ways to communicate.

Spend time talking about each individual's strengths, empowering the group to acknowledge differences as essential ingredients in collaboration rather than as roadblocks to avoid.

How are we different?

Establish a clear, flexible process.

Norms for how the group will begin its work can be established and then revisited as more information is gathered.

How will we use time?

Be accountable.

Evaluation data, collected across time as the group is working, provides concrete evidence of the extent to which the group's decisions are having the desired results.

How can we know if things are working?

Consider the context.

Problems are different, people are different, and places are different. Collaborations must be informed by the local environment rather than imported or imposed.

How is our situation unique?

Strategies for Building Community	• Begin with a news-from-home session, where members tell about things happening in their lives after school. • Begin with a news-from-my-classroom session, where members briefly share one success they have experienced since the group's last meeting. • Ask members to give book talks, either from their own recreational reading or from new children's literature. • Use a mental team-building exercise. Board games like Pictionary, Scruples, or Scattergories are naturals.
Strategies for Grappling with Ideas	• Start meetings with a recap of the previous session's content, including any cognitive conflicts that were revealed, and then set goals for the day's session. • Set up norms for brainstorming. Target sharing of as many ideas as possible, then sorting ideas into action categories—"consider now," "consider in the future." • Set up norms for discussion. Include turn taking, note taking, and periodic summarization. • Set up norms for discussing readings. Begin by addressing the authors' argument, referring directly to the text, to establish a shared understanding. Then move to participants' response to those ideas. Focus attention on what is similar to previous ideas and what is different.
Strategies for Finding Common Ground	• Provide a common lesson plan that all team members can implement individually, with a follow-up discussion about what they learned. • Use one team member's class profile (with achievement data) as a case study, assigning each group member responsibility for planning one aspect of instruction. • Use classroom videos from some or all members of the team to illustrate an issue. Allow each teacher who was video-recorded to debrief fully before a more open discussion.
Strategies for Applying Ideas	• Engage in lesson study, which takes real examples from the classrooms and engages the group in problem solving to improve the plan, to improve the implementation, or to make either planning or implementation easier. • Think through how to adapt a lesson plan to a different grade level, achievement profile, or teacher. • Consider ideas for sharing responsibility for planning lessons or for organizing materials to make the initial trial implementation smoother or easier.
Strategies for Setting New Goals	• Set a new goal that builds on successes, or one that provides a deeper look at a new conflict that has emerged. • Begin a second collaborative cycle with data analysis. If data drive the new focus, then no one member of the team is imposing a goal on others.

FIGURE 8.2: Advice on how to support collaboration at the district level from Walpole and Najera (2013, p. 525), based on Dooner, Manzuk, and Clifton (2007)
Note. From "Improving the School Reading Program: A New Call for Collaboration" by S. Walpole and K. Najera, 2013. In B. M. Taylor and N. K. Duke (Eds), *Handbook of Effective Literacy Instruction: Research-Based Practice K–8*, (p. 525), New York: The Guilford Press. Copyright 2013 by the Guilford Press. Reprinted with permission.

Concluding Thoughts: Back to the Beginning

Finding ways to make project-based instruction professionally manageable is so important—and so worth it. To remind yourself why, I end by asking you to revisit the beginning of this book. I hope that will remind you of the considerable research and theory that supports project-based instruction, the many advantages this kind of teaching holds over traditional instruction, and the compelling projects in which students can engage. My very best wishes to you as you get "inside information."

Project-Based Unit Planning Template

Project Name: _____ Project Developer(s): _____ Number of Sessions: _____

Project/Students' Purpose: _____ Audience: _____ Final Product: _____

Focal Genre(s): _____ Domain(s): _____ Key Standards: _____

	Text	Whole-Class Lesson	Small-Group, Partner, and Individual Work	Whole-Class Wrap-Up	Standards Addressed
Project Launch (Session 1)					
Reading and Research Phase*					
Session 2					
Session 3					
Session 4					
Session 5 (add sessions as needed)					
Writing and Research Phase*					
Session 6					
Session 7					
Session 8					
Session 9					
Session 10 (add sessions as needed)					

Text	Whole-Class Lesson	Small-Group, Partner, and Individual Work	Whole-Class Wrap-Up	Standards Addressed
Revision and Editing Phase				
Session 11				
Session 12				
Session 13				
Session 14				
Session 15 (add sessions as needed)				
Presentation and Celebration				

*A reminder that the phases are not rigid. Some writing will occur during Reading and Research and some reading will occur during Writing and Research.

Permission to photocopy this chart is granted to purchasers of this book for personal use only (see copyright page for details). Download this template at http://umich.edu/~nkduke/.

Appendix B

Sample Project-Based Unit Planning Sheet

Project Name: Conserving a Local Ecosystem Proposal   **Project Developer(s):** Nell Duke and Ellen Daughtery Durr   **Number of Sessions:** 15

Project/Students' Purpose: Study problems associated with local ecosystem and create a proposal for solution(s) to conserve it   **Audience:** City council and community members   **Final Product:** Hard copies of individual proposals and digital presentation of collective proposal

Focal Genre(s): Persuasive, Proposal   **Domain(s):** Science   **Key Standards:** CCSS: RI.5.6, W.5.1, W.5.5, W.5.6, W.5.8, L.1, L.2; NextGEN secondarily

Note: If possible, visit the local ecosystem prior to the start of the unit.

	Text	Whole-Class Lesson	Small-Group, Partner, and Individual Work	Whole-Class Wrap-Up	Standards Addressed
Project Launch (Session 1)	Launch Text: Students Strive to Save the Bay!	• Read Launch Text aloud • Discuss the main ideas in the text and how they are supported by key details. • Launch the unit: Connect inspirational story of people in the Launch Text to students being able to make a difference in an ecosystem near them. Describe the project. Presenting their proposal to help conserve a local ecosystem [identify that system] at a city council meeting. • Tell students they will write a summary of the Launch Text. Tell students they will use the summary to help inspire ideas for their proposal.	Have students write a summary of the Launch Text Description of ecosystem and main ideas and key supporting details. Differentiation: Support: Create a Summary graphic organizer and work with a small group to complete it. Challenge: Do additional online research on the group featured in the Launch Text.	• Ask: How did identifying the main ideas in the Launch Text help you write a summary of it? • Ask: What strategies did people in the Chesapeake Bay project use that we could consider using to help conserve our ecosystem?	RI.5.2 Determine two or more main ideas of a text and explain how they are supported by key details; summarize the text.

Reading and Research Phase*

	Text	Whole-Class Lesson	Small-Group, Partner, and Individual Work	Whole-Class Wrap-Up	Standards Addressed
Session 2	Source Text 1: "Ecosystem Threats"	• Have students read the Source Text • Ask questions to guide students in identifying the type of ecosystem in which they live. • Explain to students that their task today is to describe their local ecosystem and write a description of threats to it on the Problems graphic organizer. This will help them with their proposal to conserve the ecosystem. • Explain that to learn about the ecosystem and threats to it, students will need to search and evaluate the trustworthiness of websites. Brainstorm a list of key words for Internet searches on this topic. Review the WWDOT process from Unit 1.	• Have students work on a description of the ecosystem and ecosystem threats/problems graphic organizer • Pull together a small group to work on strategies for cracking unfamiliar words Differentiation Support: Guide students' research by providing a list of question starters: What is the threat? Why is that a threat? Challenge: Explore threats to the local ecosystem in greater depth. Think about: How long has this been perceived as a threat? Who has identified it as a threat? What other threats have been resolved, and how?	• List threats/problems identified by students in their searches • Project the "Ecosystems Threats" Source Text and ask, "How do the threats you found fit with the threats listed in this text?"	RI.5.7 Draw on information from multiple print or digital sources, demonstrating the ability to locate an answer to a question quickly or to solve a problem efficiently. W.5.7 Conduct short research projects that use several sources to build knowledge through investigation of different aspects of a topic.
Session 3	Source Text 2: "Saving the Everglades: No More Sugarcane!" Source Text 3: "Sustainable Everglades Sugarcane Production Is Possible!"	• Teach a lesson on the value of rereading. Model with one of the websites students used in Session 2. • Explain that in talking about an issue, such as problems facing the ecosystem, there will be several different points of view about how to fix it.	• Have students read the two Source Texts, and think about the different points of view they present about the sugarcane industry in the Everglades. • Review the whole-group lesson with small groups or individuals as needed.	• Engage students in a discussion comparing and contrasting the points of view represented in the two Source Texts	RI.5.6 Analyze multiple accounts of the same event or topic, noting important similarities and differences in the point of view they represent.
Session 4	Source Text 2: "Saving the Everglades: No More Sugarcane!" Source Text 3: "Sustainable Everglades Sugarcane Production Is Possible!"	• Review the two points of view on sugar cane in the Everglades • Tell students that today they will complete a graphic organizer comparing the two points of view. That will help them get used to thinking about multiple points of view on conservation; they will need to consider multiple points of view in writing their ecosystem proposal. • Model how to use the main ideas and supporting details in the text to complete a comparison chart.	• Have students create and complete their own comparison charts for the two sugarcane Source Texts Differentiation Support: Help students identify the main categories for comparison by working together to highlight the main ideas in the sugarcane articles Challenge: Focus on the persuasive elements used by the writers of the sugarcane articles and add them to the chart (e.g., persuasive language, claim, evidence).	• Have partners share their charts and talk about the position they each most agreed with • Reveal that the next class will feature a guest speaker who will talk about possible solutions for the threats to the local ecosystem	RI.5.6 Analyze multiple accounts of the same event or topic, noting important similarities and differences in the point of view they represent.

Session	Text	Whole-Class Lesson	Small-Group/Partner and Individual Work	Whole-Class Wrap-Up	Standards Addressed
Session 5 (add sessions as needed)		• Instruct students on how to take notes on the Ecosystem Solutions graphic organizer as they listen to the speaker. • Introduce the guest speaker. • Have students take notes as they listen to the speaker.	• Have students work in pairs to review and expand on their notes (after the speaker leaves). Differentiation: Support: Invite students to listen to a recording of the guest speaker and fill in missing information on the Ecosystem Solutions graphic organizer. Challenge: Ask students to write a thank-you note to the speaker for coming to the classroom.	• Have students draw on their notes to help generate a list of possible solutions to go with the previous list of problems/threats. • Sign and send the thank-you note to the speaker.	W 5.8 Recall relevant information from experiences or gather relevant information from print and digital sources; summarize or paraphrase information in notes and finished work and provide a list of sources. SL 5.3 Summarize the points a speaker makes and explain how each claim is supported by reasons and evidence.

Writing and Research Phase*

Session	Text	Whole-Class Lesson	Small-Group/Partner and Individual Work	Whole-Class Wrap-Up	Standards Addressed
Session 6	Mentor Text: Protecting Jakarta's Coastline: A Proposal	• Read aloud the text. • Write down and explain the following terms from the text: evidence, counterargument, rebuttal. • Discuss the similarities between Adeline Suwana's process in working to protect the Jakarta coastline with students' process in working to protect their local ecosystem.	• Have groups write the structure of the proposal in the Mentor Text on the Proposal Structure graphic organizers. Differentiation: Support: Encourage students to use sticky notes to label the proposal elements in the Mentor Text before writing the full structure. Challenge: Examine the language and graphics in the Mentor Text proposal.	• Create a class list of the elements of the proposal in the Mentor Text. Discuss how each element contributes to the text's effectiveness.	RI 5.1 Quote accurately from a text when explaining what the text says explicitly and when drawing inferences from the text.
Session 7	Mentor Text: Protecting Jakarta's Coastline: A Proposal	• Review the explanation of evidence from Session 6. Explain that evidence is used to support reasons, which makes a writer's opinion even more persuasive. Give some examples: using a direct quotation, reporting the results of a survey, and so on. • Guide students in identifying the evidence in the Mentor Text that supports the writer's opinion. Ask: How does this evidence strengthen Adeline Suwana's opinion?	• Have students use their completed Ecosystem Problems and Ecosystem Solutions graphic organizers to formulate opinions, reasons, and evidence for their proposals. Have students use a graphic organizer for this purpose. Differentiation: Support: Have students work with a partner to formulate their opinions, reasons, and evidence. Challenge: Prepare questions for an interview with another expert who has knowledge of the local ecosystem (e.g., a botanist or geologist from the college).	• Have partners share their ideas for opinions, reasons, and evidence, and offer feedback about whether the evidence supports the reasons behind their opinions.	W 5.8 Recall relevant information from experiences or gather relevant information from print and digital sources; summarize or paraphrase information in notes and finished work and provide a list of sources.

	Text	Whole-Class Lesson	Small-Group, Partner, and Individual Work	Whole-Class Wrap-Up	Standards Addressed
Session 8	Launch Text: Students Strive to Save the Bay!	• Tell students they'll start writing their individual proposals today. • Review the elements of a proposal charted in Session 6. • Discuss the importance of an introduction that will grab a reader's attention immediately. Read aloud/ discuss the introduction to the proposal in the Mentor Text. Point out that the introduction presents the writer's opinion. • Remind students of the importance of supporting their reasons with evidence. Tell students that their proposals should contain at least three reasons and evidence to support each one.	• Have individuals work from their opinion, reasons, and evidence notes from the previous session, plus their original notes and graphic organizers, to begin to write their drafts. Differentiation: Support: Encourage students to use a highlighter to mark evidence in their notes. Challenge: Add sidebars to their drafts to provide interesting facts about the local ecosystem.	• Share a particularly well organized/ structured draft. • If time permits, ask pairs to share their proposal drafts thus far and give feedback on the organization and structure.	W 5.1 Write opinion pieces on topics or texts, supporting a point of view with reasons and information. a. Introduce a topic or text clearly, state an opinion, and create an organizational structure in which ideas are logically grouped to support the writer's purpose. b. Provide logically ordered reasons that are supported by facts and details. c. Link opinion and reasons using words, phrases, and clauses (e.g., *consequently, specifically*). Craft: Organize information.
Session 9	Launch Text: Students Strive to Save the Bay! Mentor Text: Protecting Jakarta's Coastline: A Proposal	• Review the terms *counterargument* and *rebuttal* from Session 6. Read and discuss the counterargument and rebuttal in the proposal in the Mentor Text. • Ask: Why might someone disagree with the opinion in your proposal, even though it's backed up by reasons and evidence? • Explain that today students will decide on a counterargument and rebuttal for it. Encourage them to use the language structure in their proposals: "Some people may argue _____ [counterargument], but _____ [rebuttal]."	• Have individuals list 3 to 5 counterarguments and then choose one to rebut. • Have them continue their drafts by adding a counterargument/rebuttal section. Differentiation: Support: Provide a written copy of the suggested language structure for students to use. Challenge: Write at least three different examples of counterargument/rebuttal. Choose the strongest to include in the proposal.	• Share a particularly strong counterargument and rebuttal. • If time permits, ask pairs to share their counterargument and rebuttal, and provide feedback.	W 5.1 Write opinion pieces on topics or texts, supporting a point of view with reasons and information. a. Introduce a topic or text clearly, state an opinion, and create an organizational structure in which ideas are logically grouped to support the writer's purpose. b. Provide logically ordered reasons that are supported by facts and details. c. Link opinion and reasons using words, phrases, and clauses (e.g., *consequently, specifically*). Craft: Be interesting. Keep your reader's attention.
Session 10 (add sessions as needed)	Mentor Text: Protecting Jakarta's Coastline: A Proposal	• Conduct a lesson based on a problem seen in students' reading and writing. • Read aloud the conclusion to the proposal in the Mentor Text. Discuss what makes the conclusion successful. If necessary, point out that the conclusion restated Adeline Suvana's opinion.	• Have students apply what they learned from the lesson to their writing. • Have individuals continue their drafts by adding a conclusion.	• Share a particularly effective conclusion. • If time permits, ask partners to share their conclusions and feedback about whether the conclusion successfully ties back into the opinion in the introduction.	W 5.1 Write opinion pieces on topics or texts, supporting a point of view with reasons and information. a. Introduce a topic or text clearly, state an opinion, and create an organizational structure in which ideas are logically grouped to support the writer's purpose. b. Provide logically ordered reasons that are supported by facts and details. c. Link opinion and reasons using words, phrases, and clauses (e.g., *consequently, specifically*).

Revision and Editing Phase

	Text	Whole-Class Lesson	Small-group, Partner, and Individual Work	Whole-Class Wrap-Up	Standards Addressed
Session 11	Mentor Text: Protecting Jakarta's Coastline: A Proposal	• Discuss how graphics—photos, charts, graphs, and diagrams—can make proposals even stronger. Show examples from the proposal in the Mentor Text and other resources. • Remind students how to find trustworthy sources on the Internet.	• Have individuals add to their drafts by selecting and adding graphics. • Have students complete a Self-Reflection Form. Differentiation: Support: Help students brainstorm search terms for graphics that might relate to their proposals. Challenge: Create a data graphic to add to the proposals (e.g., a circle graph showing results of a poll or a line graph showing the decreasing number of a species in the ecosystem over time).	• Share some particularly effective graphics. • If time permits, ask partners to share their graphics and give feedback on their effectiveness. (After session: Give students' drafts and Volunteer Feedback Forms to community members who have volunteered to read and comment on them. Fill out a Teacher Feedback Form for each proposal. Draft an oral and digital presentation using pieces of each student's proposal. [Note: If you have more sessions available, have students play a greater role in developing the digital presentation.]	W.5.4 Produce clear and coherent writing in which the development and organization are appropriate to the task, purpose, and audience. Craft: Use graphics.
Session 12		• Remind students of the purpose and audience for their proposals. Explain that today they will work on presenting their proposals orally. • Share key guidelines about speaking in front of an audience: Maintain eye contact; use a strong voice; be engaging. • Model some positive and negative examples of speaking in front of an audience. • Explain that you have created a group proposal for presentation at the city council meeting by selecting pieces of each student's proposal. Indicate which piece each student will present.	• Have students practice their pieces first individually and then in small groups, offering feedback to one another. Differentiation: Support: Create a chart for the key guidelines using icons (e.g., an eye, an open mouth, a smiling mouth, or gesturing hands). Challenge: Look online for additional guidance about effective public speaking. Prepare a poster for everyone's reference.	• Ask students to discuss what they learned from the presentation practice. (Collect feedback forms from the volunteers. Attach each student's Volunteer and Teacher Feedback Forms to his/her proposal draft.) Remind students to practice their part of the oral presentation at home.)	W.5.5 With guidance and support from peers and adults, develop and strengthen writing as needed by planning, revising, editing, rewriting, or trying a new approach. SL.5.4 Report on a topic or text or present an opinion, sequencing ideas logically and using appropriate facts and relevant, descriptive details to support main ideas or themes; speak clearly at an understandable pace. Craft: Clean, clear writing.
Session 13	Mentor Text: Protecting Jakarta's Coastline: A Proposal	• Return proposal drafts with feedback forms. Point out the importance of the volunteers' feedback; as community members, they are part of the target audience.	• Have individuals revise based on Self-Reflection Forms and other's feedback. Differentiation: Support: Help students focus on the area most in need of revision. Guide them in comparing the feedback forms to find areas of common concern. Challenge: Look for sections that could use more persuasive elements or language.	• Share examples of particularly effective revisions students have made. • If time permits, ask partners to share how they used the feedback forms in revising their writing.	W.5.5 With guidance and support from peers and adults, develop and strengthen writing as needed by planning, revising, editing, rewriting, or trying a new approach. Craft: Clean, clear writing.

Text	Whole-Class Lesson	Small-Group, Partner, and Individual Work	Whole-Class Wrap-Up	Standards Addressed
Session 14	• Go over Editing Checklist with students. • Review the list of proposal elements	• Have individuals reread their proposals, pausing frequently to ensure that grammar, punctuation, and spelling reflect their best efforts. • Have them edit their proposals using the Editing Checklist. Differentiation: Support: Help students focus on editing one page at a time. Challenge: Encourage students to edit one another's work.	• Share examples of edits students have made. • Have students turn and talk about an edit they made and why they made it. • Remind students to practice their part of the oral presentation at home.	L.1 Demonstrate command of the conventions of standard English grammar and usage when writing or speaking. L.2 Demonstrate command of the conventions of standard English capitalization, punctuation, and spelling when writing. Craft: Clean, clear writing
Session 15 (add sessions as needed)	• Have students run through the presentation as a whole group. • Explain to students that today they will create the final copy of their individual proposals.	• Have individuals create the final copy of their proposals. Differentiation: Support: Video-record students presenting their parts so they can watch and look for areas to improve. Challenge: Research other subjects on the council meeting agenda	• Talk through the logistics of transportation and the meeting (or of the city council members' visit to the school). • If time allows, run through the presentation again.	W.5.6 With some guidance and support from adults, use technology, including the Internet, to produce and publish writing as well as to interact and collaborate with others; demonstrate sufficient command of keyboarding skills to type a minimum of two pages in a single sitting. Craft: Clean, clear writing

Presentation and Celebration

Presentation

- Present at a city council meeting if possible. Distribute individual proposals to council members and other members of the audience.
- Alternatively, invite members of the city council and/or larger community to listen to the presentation in the classroom.
- Arrange to have the presentation recorded and post it online for students

Celebration

- Enjoy refreshments with members of the city council or community following the presentation.
- Invite people who have careers involving the environment to hear the presentation and speak to the class about their field experience.

*A reminder that the phases are not rigid. Some writing will occur during Reading and Research and some reading will occur during Writing and Research.

Permission to photocopy this chart is granted to purchasers of this book for personal use only (see copyright page for details).

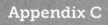

Sample Informational Text
Reading and Writing Interest Survey

Please note: Categories listed on the survey on the next two pages could be altered to tap categories that you think are particularly appropriate to the age of your students, that you are particularly wondering about, or that seem particularly current or relevant to your standards or location.

If you are working with early elementary students, you might also alter the wording to include read-aloud and shared writing so children still feel that the items apply to them. Also, you should read the survey to children and transcribe their responses. You could also consider sending the survey home to complete with families (working in class with students whose families cannot support them in this).

Name: _____ **Date:** _____

I want to learn more about what you do and don't like to read and write. Please tell me how you really feel. It's okay if you don't like every kind of reading and writing.

What are some things you like to read and write about?

_____

_____

_____

What are some things you don't like to read and write about?

_____

_____

_____

Please circle all of the kinds of things you like to read or watch:

Fictional Picture Books	Newspapers	Comic Books
Informational Picture Books	Websites	Manga
Chapter Books	Videos	Textbooks
Encyclopedias	TV Shows	
Magazines	Dictionaries	

Please circle all of the topics you like to read and/or write about:

Ocean Animals	Computers	Building
Land Animals	Machines	How Things Work
Pets	Geology/Rocks	Art
The Human Body	Famous People	Music
Plants	Famous Scientists	Movies
Space	Famous Explorers	Plays
The Earth	Famous Inventors	Weather
Natural Disasters (tornadoes, earthquakes . . .)	Famous Leaders	History/Olden Times
	Famous Authors	Transportation (cars, trucks, trains . . .)
Countries Around the World	Famous Children	
Places in the United States	True Stories	Sports
Dinosaurs	Arts and Crafts	Social Studies
Ancient (very old) Egypt, Rome, Greece	Cooking	Farming

Is there anything else you would like to tell me about what you like to read and write about?

_____

_____

_____

_____

_____

Professional References Cited

Ainley, M. (2006). Connecting with learning: Motivation, affect, and cognition in interest processes. *Educational Psychology Review, 18*(4), 391–405.

Anderson, E. (1998). *Motivational and cognitive influences on conceptual knowledge: The combination of science observation and interesting texts.* (Unpublished doctoral dissertation). University of Maryland, College Park.

Baumann, J. F., & Bergeron, B. S. (1993). Story map instruction using children's literature: Effects on first graders' comprehension of central narrative elements. *Journal of Reading Behavior, 25*(4), 407–437.

Baumann, J. F., Edwards, E. C., Boland, E. M., Olejnik, S., & Kame'enui, E. J. (2003). Vocabulary tricks: Effects of instruction in morphology and context on fifth-grade students' ability to derive and infer word meanings. *American Educational Research Journal, 40*, 447–494.

Beck, I. L., & McKeown, M. G. (2007). Increasing young low-income children's oral vocabulary repertoires through rich and focused instruction. *The Elementary School Journal, 107*(3), 251–271.

Block, M. K. (2013). *The impact of identifying a specific purpose and external audience for writing on second graders' writing quality.* (Unpublished doctoral dissertation). Michigan State University, East Lansing.

Boaler, J. (1998). Open and closed mathematics: Student experiences and understandings. *Journal for Research in Mathematics Education, 29*, 41–62.

Bodrova, E., & Leong, D. J. (1998). Scaffolding emergent writing in the zone of proximal development. *Literacy Teaching and Learning, 3*(2), 1–18.

Brinkerhoff, E. H., & Roehrig, A. D. (2014). *No more sharpening pencils during work time and other time wasters.* Portsmouth, NH: Heinemann.

Cahill, C., Horvath, K., McGill-Franzen, A., & Allington, R. (2013). *No more summer-reading loss.* Portsmouth, NH: Heinemann.

Carney, R. N., & Levin, J. R. (2002). Pictorial illustrations still improve students' learning from text. *Educational Psychology Review, 14*, 5–26.

Cassetta, G., & Sawyer, B. (2013). *No more taking away recess and other problematic discipline practices.* Portsmouth, NH: Heinemann.

Caswell, L. J., & Duke, N. K. (1998). Non-narrative as a catalyst for literacy development. *Language Arts, 75*, 108–117.

Cervetti, G. N., Barber, J., Dorph, R., Pearson, P. D., & Goldschmidt, P. G. (2012). The impact of an integrated approach to science and literacy in elementary school classrooms. *Journal of Research in Science Teaching, 49*, 631–658.

Cohen, M., & Riel, M. (1989). The effect of distant audiences on students' writing. *American Educational Research Journal, 26,* 143–159.

Craig, S. A. (2003). The effects of an adapted interactive writing intervention on kindergarten children's phonological awareness, spelling, and early reading development. *Reading Research Quarterly, 38*(4), 438–440.

Crowhurst, M., & Piche, G. L. (1979). Audience and mode of discourse effects on syntactic complexity in writing at two grade levels. *Research in the Teaching of English, 13,* 101–109.

Culham, R. (2003). *6+1 traits of writing: The complete guide.* New York: Scholastic.

Dewey, J. (1902). *The child and the curriculum.* Chicago: University of Chicago Press.

Dougherty Stahl, K. A. (2008). The effects of three instructional methods on the reading comprehension and content acquisition of novice readers. *Journal of Literacy Research, 40,* 359–93.

Dressel, J. (1990). The effects of listening to and discussing different qualities of children's literature on the narrative writing of fifth graders. *Research in the Teaching of English, 24,* 397–414.

Duke, N. K. (2000). 3.6 minutes per day: The scarcity of informational texts in first grade. *Reading Research Quarterly, 35,* 202–224.

Duke, N. K., & Bennett-Armistead, V. S., with Huxley, A., Johnson, M., McLurkin, D., Roberts, E., Rosen, C., Vogel, E. (2003). *Reading and writing informational text in the primary grades: Research-based practices.* New York: Scholastic.

Duke, N. K., Caughlan, S., Juzwik, M. M., & Martin, N. M. (2012). *Reading and writing genre with purpose in K–8 classrooms.* Portsmouth, NH: Heinemann.

Duke, N. K., & Halvorsen, A-L. (in progress). *Scaling up a promising approach to narrowing the SES achievement gap in primary-grade social studies and content literacy.* [Research project].

Duke, N. K., & Kays, J. (1998). "Can I say 'Once upon a time'?": Kindergarten children developing knowledge of information book language. *Early Childhood Research Quarterly, 13,* 295–318.

Duke, N. K., Norman, R. R., Roberts, K. L., Martin, N. M., Knight, J. A., Morsink, P. M., & Calkins, S. L. (2013). Beyond concepts of print: Development of concepts of graphics in text, pre-K to grade 3. *Research in the Teaching of English, 48,* 175–203.

Duke, N. K., & Pearson, P. D. (2002). Effective practices for developing reading comprehension. In A. E. Farstrup & S. J. Samuels (Eds.), *What research has to say about reading instruction* (3rd ed.) (pp. 205–242). Newark, DE: International Reading Association.

Duke, N. K., Pearson, P. D., Strachan, S. L., & Billman, A. K. (2011). Essential elements of fostering and teaching reading comprehension. In S. J. Samuels & A. E. Farstrup (Eds.), *What research has to say about reading instruction* (4th ed.) (pp. 51–93). Newark, DE: International Reading Association.

Duke, N. K., Purcell-Gates, V., Hall, L. A., & Tower, C. (2006/2007). Authentic literacy activities for developing comprehension and writing. *The Reading Teacher, 60*, 344–355.

Duke, N. K., & Roberts, K. M. (2010). The genre-specific nature of reading comprehension. In D. Wyse, R. Andrews & J. Hoffman (Eds.), *The Routledge international handbook of English language and literacy teaching* (pp. 74–86). London: Routledge.

Duke, N. K., & Watanabe, L. M. (2013). Reading and writing specific genres. In B. M. Taylor & N. K. Duke (Eds.), *Handbook of effective literacy instruction: Research-based practice K–8* (pp. 346–368). New York: Guilford.

Elleman, A. M., Lindo, E. J., Morphy, P., & Compton, D. L. (2009). The impact of vocabulary instruction on passage-level comprehension of school-age children: A meta-analysis. *Journal of Research on Educational Effectiveness, 2*(1), 1–44.

Filippatou, D., & Kaldi, S. (2010). The effectiveness of project-based learning on pupils with learning difficulties regarding academic performance, group work, and motivation. *International Journal of Special Education, 25*, 17–26.

Fingeret, L. (2008). March of the penguins: Building knowledge in a kindergarten classroom. *The Reading Teacher, 62*, 96–103.

Fingeret, L. (2012). *Graphics in children's informational texts: A content analysis.* (Unpublished doctoral dissertation). Michigan State University, East Lansing.

Gersten, R., Fuchs, L., Williams, J., & Baker, S. (2001). Teaching reading comprehension strategies to students with learning disabilities: A review of research. *Review of Educational Research, 71*, 279–320.

Graham, S., Bollinger, A., Booth Olson, C., D'Aoust, C., MacArthur, C., McCutchen, D., & Olinghouse, N. (2012). *Teaching elementary school students to be effective writers: A practice guide* (NCEE 2012-4058). Washington, DC: National Center for Education Evaluation and Regional Assistance, Institute of Education Sciences, U.S. Department of Education. Retrieved from http://ies.ed.gov/ncee/ wwc/ publications_reviews.aspx#pubsearch

Graham, S., & Harris, K. (1989). Improving learning disabled students' skills at composing essays: Self-instructional strategy training. *Exceptional Children, 56*, 201–214.

Graham, S., & Hebert, M. (2011). Writing to read: A meta-analysis of the impact of writing and writing instruction on reading. *Harvard Educational Review, 81*(4), 710–744.

Graham, S., McKeown, D., Kiuhara, S., & Harris, K. R. (2012). A meta-analysis of writing instruction for students in the elementary grades. *Journal of Educational Psychology, 104*, 879–896.

Graham, S., & Sandmel, K. (2011). The process writing approach: A meta-analysis. *The Journal of Educational Research, 104*, 396–407.

Guthrie, J. T., McRae, A., & Klauda, S. L. (2007). Contributions of Concept-Oriented Reading Instruction to knowledge about interventions for motivations in reading. *Educational Psychologist, 42*(4), 237–250.

Halvorsen, A., Duke, N. K., Brugar, K. A., Block, M. K., Strachan, S. L., Berka, M. B., & Brown, J. M. (2012). Narrowing the achievement gap in second-grade social studies and content area literacy: The promise of a project-based approach. *Theory and Research in Social Education, 40,* 198–229.

Harvey, S., & Daniels, H. (2009). *Comprehension and collaboration: Inquiry circles in action.* Portsmouth, NH: Heinemann.

Heick, T. (2013, February 9). The gradual release of responsibility model in 6 simple words [blog]. Retrieved from http://www.teachthought.com/teaching/the-gradual-release-of-responsibility-model-in-6-simple-words

Hernandez-Ramos, P., & De La Paz, S. (2009). Learning history in middle school by designing multimedia in a project-based learning experience. *Journal of Research on Technology in Education, 42,* 151–173.

Hertzog, N. B. (2007). Transporting pedagogy: Implementing the project approach in two first-grade classrooms. *Journal of Academic Achievement, 18,* 530–564.

Jeong, J. S., Gaffney, J. S., & Choi, J. O. (2010). Availability and use of informational text in second, third, and fourth grades. *Research in the Teaching of English, 44,* 435–456.

Jiménez, L. M., & Duke, N. K. (2014). *The effect of high and low interest on informational text reading comprehension in elementary-age readers.* (Unpublished manuscript). Boston University.

Juzwik, M. M. (2009). *The rhetoric of teaching: Understanding the dynamics of Holocaust narratives in an English classroom.* Cresskill, NJ: Hampton Press.

Kaldi, S., Filippatou, D., & Govaris, C. (2011). Project-based learning in primary schools: Effects on pupils' learning and attitudes. *Education 3–13: International Journal of Primary, Elementary and Early Years Education, 39*(1), 35–47.

Kays, J., & Duke, N. K. (1998). Getting students into information books. *Teaching PreK–8, 29*(2), 52–54.

Keene, E. O. (2008). *To understand: New horizons in reading comprehension.* Portsmouth, NH: Heinemann.

Keene, E. O. (2012). *Talk about understanding: Rethinking classroom talk to enhance comprehension.* Portsmouth, NH: Heinemann.

Kilpatrick, W.H. (1918). The project method: The use of the purposeful act in the educative process. *Teachers College Record, 19,* 319–334.

Kim, J. S., & Quinn, D. M. (2013). The effects of summer reading on low-income children's literacy achievement from kindergarten to grade 8: A meta-analysis of classroom and home interventions. *Review of Educational Research, 83,* 386–431.

Kucan, L., & Beck, I. L. (1997). Thinking aloud and reading comprehension research: Inquiry, instruction, and social interaction. *Review of Educational Research, 67*(3), 271–299.

Langer, J. A. (1995). *Envisioning literature: Literary understanding and literature instruction.* New York: Teachers College Press.

Martin, N. M. (2011). *Exploring informational text comprehension: Reading biography, persuasive text, and procedural text in the elementary grades.* (Unpublished doctoral dissertation). Michigan State University, East Lansing.

Miller, D., & Moss, B. (2013). *No more independent reading without support.* Portsmouth, NH: Heinemann.

Moje, E. B. (2008). Foregrounding the disciplines in secondary literacy teaching and learning: A call for change. *Journal of Adolescent and Adult Literacy, 52*(2), 96–107.

Moll, L. C., Amanti, C., Neff, D., & Gonzalez, N. (1992). Funds of knowledge for teaching: Using a qualitative approach to connect homes and classrooms. *Theory into Practice, 31,* 132–141.

Monte-Sano, C. (2012). Build skills by doing history. *Phi Delta Kappan, 94*(3), 62–65.

Morphy, P., & Graham, S. (2012). Word processing programs and weaker writers/readers: A meta-analysis of research findings. *Reading and Writing, 25,* 641–678.

Morrow, L. M. (1984). Reading stories to young children: Effects of story structure and traditional questioning strategies on comprehension. *Journal of Reading Behavior, 16*(4), 273–288.

Murphy, P. K., Wilkinson, I. A. G., Soter, A. O., Hennessey, M. N., & Alexander, J. F. (2009). Examining the effects of classroom discussion on students' comprehension of text: A meta-analysis. *Journal of Educational Psychology, 101,* 740–764.

National Governors Association Center for Best Practices & Council of Chief State School Officers. (2010). Common Core State Standards for English Language Arts and Literacy in History/Social Studies, Science, and Technical Subjects. Washington D.C.: National Governors Association Center for Best Practices, Council of Chief State School Officers.

Okolo, C. M., & Ferretti, R. P. (1996). Knowledge acquisition and technology-supported projects in the social studies for students with learning disabilities. *Journal of Special Education Technology, 13,* 91–103.

Olinghouse, N. G., & Wilson, J. (2013). The relationship between vocabulary and writing quality in three genres. *Reading and Writing: An Interdisciplinary Journal, 26,* 45–65.

Pappas, C. C. (2006). The information book genre: Its role in integrated science literacy research and practice. *Reading Research Quarterly, 41,* 226–250.

Parker, W., Mosborg, S., Bransford, J., Vye, N., Wilkerson, J., & Abbott, R. (2011). Rethinking advanced high school coursework: Tackling the depth/breadth tension in the AP US Government and Politics course. *Journal of Curriculum Studies, 43,* 533–559.

Partnership for 21st Century Skills. (n.d.). Framework for 21st century learning. Retrieved April 10, 2014, from http://www.p21.org/about-us/p21-framework

Pearson, P. D., & Gallagher, M. C. (1983). The instruction of reading comprehension. *Contemporary Educational Psychology, 8*(3), 317–344.

Pressley, M., Wharton-McDonald, R., Allington, R., Block, C. C., Morrow, L., Tracey, D., et al. (2001). A study of effective first-grade literacy instruction. *Scientific Studies of Reading, 5*(1), 35-58.

Purcell-Gates, V., Duke, N. K., & Martineau, J. A. (2007). Learning to read and write genre-specific text: Roles of authentic experience and explicit teaching. *Reading Research Quarterly, 42*, 8–45.

Puzio, K., & Colby, G. T. (2013). Cooperative learning and literacy: A meta-analytic review. *Journal of Research on Educational Effectiveness, 6*, 339–360.

Recht, D. R., & Leslie, L. (1988). Effects of prior knowledge on good and poor reader's memory of text. *Journal of Educational Psychology, 80*, 16–20.

Riddle Buly, M., & Valencia, S. W. (2002). Below the bar: Profiles of students who fail state reading assessments. *Educational Evaluation and Policy Analysis, 24*, 219–239.

Rivet, A. E., & Krajcik, J. S. (2004). Achieving standards in urban systemic reform: An example of a sixth grade project-based science curriculum. *Journal of Research in Science Teaching, 41*, 669–692.

Robb, L. (2004). *Nonfiction writing from the inside out: Writing lessons inspired by conversations with leading authors.* New York: Scholastic.

Roberts, K. L., Norman, R. R., Duke, N. K., Morsink, P., Martin, N. M., & Knight, J. A. (2013). Diagrams, timelines, and tables—oh my! Concepts and comprehension of graphics. *The Reading Teacher, 61*, 12–24.

Roth, K., & Guinee, K. (2011). Ten minutes a day: The impact of interactive writing instruction on first graders' independent writing. *Journal of Early Childhood Literacy, 11*, 331–361.

Rowe, D. W. (March 29, 2011). Scaffolded writing. Retrieved from https://sites.google.com/site/deborahwellsrowe/home

Scanlon, D. M., Anderson, K. L., & Sweeney, J. M. (2010). *Early intervention for reading difficulties: The interactive strategies approach.* New York: Guilford.

Schumaker, J. B., Deshler, D. D., Alley, G. R., Warner, M. W., Clark, F. L., & Nolan, S. (1982). Error monitoring: A learning strategy for improving adolescent academic performance. In W. M. Cruickshank & J. W. Lerner (Eds.), *Coming of Age: Vol. 3* (pp. 170–183). Syracuse, NY: Syracuse University Press.

Shanahan, C., Shanahan, T., & Misischia, C. (2011). Analysis of expert readers in three disciplines: History, mathematics, and chemistry. *Journal of Literacy Research, 43*, 393–429.

Shanahan, T. (2006). Relations among oral language, reading and writing development. In C. A. MacArthur, S. Graham, & J. Fitzgerald (Eds.), *Handbook of writing research* (pp. 171–183). New York: Guilford Press.

Shanahan, T., Callison, K., Carriere, C., Duke, N. K., Pearson, P. D., Schatschneider, C., & Torgesen, J. (2010). *Improving reading comprehension in kindergarten through 3rd grade: A practice guide* (NCEE 2010-4038). Washington, DC: National Center for Education Evaluation and Regional Assistance, Institute of Education Sciences, U.S. Department of Education. Retrieved from whatworks. http://ed.gov/publications/practiceguides

Shanahan, T. (2014, May). Instructional level and text complexity. Presentation of the annual research address at the International Reading Association conference, New Orleans, LA.

Taylor, B. M. (2011). *Catching schools: An action guide to schoolwide reading improvement.* Portsmouth, NH: Heinemann.

Thomas, J. W. (2000). *A review of research on project-based learning.* San Rafael, CA: The Autodesk Foundation.

Toulmin, S. E. (1958). *The uses of argument.* Cambridge, UK: Cambridge University Press.

U. S. Department of Education, Office of Planning, Evaluation, and Policy Development. *Evaluation of the National Assessment of Educational Progress, Study Reports,* Washington, D.C., 2009.

Walpole, S., & Najera, K. (2013). Improving the school reading program: A new call for collaboration. In B. M. Taylor & N. K. Duke (Eds.), *Handbook of effective literacy instruction: Research-based practice K–8* (pp. 510–529). New York: Guilford.

Yopp, R. H., & Yopp, H. K. (2006). Informational text as read-alouds at school and home. *Journal of Literacy Research,* 38(1), 37–51.

Zhang, S., & Duke, N. K. (2011). The impact of instruction in the WWWDOT Framework on students' disposition and ability to evaluate web sites as sources of information. *The Elementary School Journal,* 112(1), 132–154.

Zhang, S., Duke, N. K., & Jiménez, L. J. (2011). The WWWDOT approach to improving students' critical evaluation of websites. *The Reading Teacher,* 65, 150–158.

Children's Books Cited

Anderson, L. (2014). Food scientist: Taste testing. In Source texts: Project: Flavored drinks recipe booklet. New York: Scholastic.

Arnosky, J. (2004). Beachcombing: Exploring the seashore. New York: Dutton Children's Books.

Beeler, S. (1998). Throw your tooth on the roof. New York: Houghton Mifflin.

Black, S. (2014). Inventors who have changed life at home. New York: Scholastic.

Carson, M. K. (2014). Eat right to be your best. New York: Scholastic.

Coutu, R. (Ed.). (2014). "If you want my opinion . . .": Letters by kids on issues that matter to kids New York: Scholastic.

Coutu, R. (2014). What is a survey? In Source texts: Project: Local Issues Op Eds. New York: Scholastic.

Dahl, R. (1961). James and the giant peach. New York: Alfred A. Knopf.

Diaz, J. R. (2014). How to interview. In Source texts: Project: School staff poster. New York: Scholastic.

Geller, K. (2014). Gross science! New York: Scholastic.

Ghiglieri, C. (2014). Questions and answers about sharks. In Source texts: Project: Endangered marine animal booklet. New York: Scholastic.

Goudarzi, S. (2014). Olympians vs. animals. In Amazing animals: A collection of articles by magazine writer Sara Goudarzi. New York: Scholastic.

Jenkins, S. (2004). Actual size. Boston: Houghton Mifflin.

McBrier, P. (2001). Beatrice's goat. New York: Atheneum.

Rathmann, P. (1995). Officer Buckle and Gloria. New York: G. P. Putnam's Sons.

Ryan, P. M. (2002). When Marian Sang: The true recital of Marian Anderson, the voice of a century. New York: Scholastic.

Selznick, B. (2007). The invention of Hugo Cabret. New York: Scholastic.

Weinberger, K. (2014). How to do chores at home. New York: Scholastic.

Winter, J. (2010). Biblioburro: A true story from Colombia. New York: Scholastic.

Index

Page numbers in italics refer to figures and tables.

About the Author

Nell K. Duke, Ed.D., is a professor of literacy, language, and culture and faculty associate in the combined program in education and psychology at the University of Michigan. Duke received her bachelor's degree from Swarthmore College and her master's and doctoral degrees from Harvard University. Duke's work focuses on early literacy development, particularly among children living in poverty. Her specific areas of expertise include the development of informational reading and writing in young children, comprehension development and instruction in early schooling, and issues of equity in literacy education.

She currently serves as a member of the International Literacy Association Literacy Research Panel and co-principal investigator on projects funded by the Institute of Education Sciences, the National Science Foundation, and the Spencer Foundation. Duke is the recipient of the P. David Pearson Scholarly Influence Award from the Literacy Research Association. She has also received the American Educational Research Association Early Career Award, the Literacy Research Association Early Career Achievement Award, the International Reading Association Dina Feitelson Research Award, the National Council of Teachers of English Promising Researcher Award, and the International Reading Association Outstanding Dissertation Award.

She is author and co-author of numerous journal articles and book chapters as well as the books *Reading and Writing Informational Text in the Primary Grades: Research-Based Practices; Literacy and the Youngest Learner: Best Practices for Educators of Children from Birth to Five; Beyond Bedtime Stories: A Parent's Guide to Promoting Reading, Writing, and Other Literacy Skills From Birth to 5; Reading and Writing Genre with Purpose in K–8 Classrooms;* and the workshop series *ABCs of Emergent Literacy* and *Engaging Families in Children's Literacy Development: A Complete Workshop Series.* She is also co-editor of the Not This, But That book series, editor of The Research-Informed Classroom book series, and co-editor of the *Handbook of Effective Literacy Instruction: Research-based Practice K to 8* and *Literacy Research Methodologies.*

Duke teaches preservice, inservice, and doctoral courses in literacy education, speaks and consults widely on literacy education, and is an active member of several literacy-related organizations. She has served as author and consultant on a number of educational programs, including Connect 4 Learning, *Buzz About IT, iOpeners, National Geographic Science K–2, DLM Express,* and, most recently, *Information in Action.*

For more about Nell K. Duke's work, see: http://umich.edu/~nkduke/.